the ULTIMATE

garage

By Jeanne Huber and the

Editors of Sunset Books

Menlo Park, California

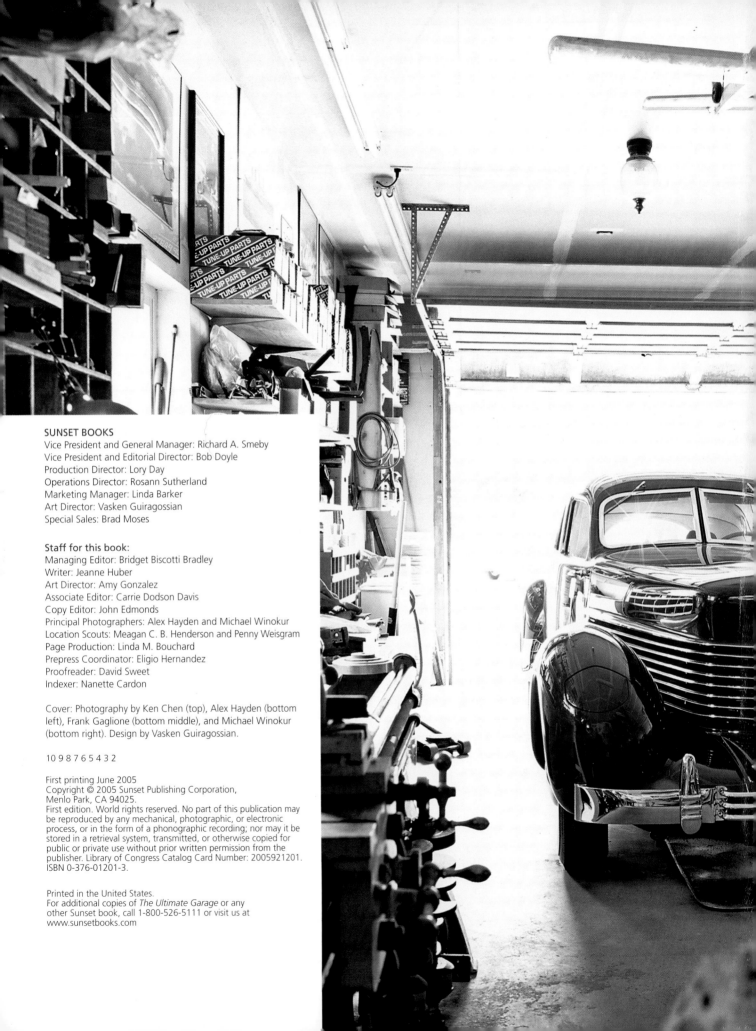

SUNSET BOOKS

Vice President and General Manager: Richard A. Smeby
Vice President and Editorial Director: Bob Doyle
Production Director: Lory Day
Operations Director: Rosann Sutherland
Marketing Manager: Linda Barker
Art Director: Vasken Guiragossian
Special Sales: Brad Moses

Staff for this book:

Managing Editor: Bridget Biscotti Bradley
Writer: Jeanne Huber
Art Director: Amy Gonzalez
Associate Editor: Carrie Dodson Davis
Copy Editor: John Edmonds
Principal Photographers: Alex Hayden and Michael Winokur
Location Scouts: Meagan C. B. Henderson and Penny Weisgram
Page Production: Linda M. Bouchard
Prepress Coordinator: Eligio Hernandez
Proofreader: David Sweet
Indexer: Nanette Cardon

Cover: Photography by Ken Chen (top), Alex Hayden (bottom
left), Frank Gaglione (bottom middle), and Michael Winokur
(bottom right). Design by Vasken Guiragossian.

10 9 8 7 6 5 4 3 2

First printing June 2005
Copyright © 2005 Sunset Publishing Corporation,
Menlo Park, CA 94025.

Printed in the United States.
For additional copies of *The Ultimate Garage* or any
other Sunset book, call 1-800-526-5111 or visit us at
www.sunsetbooks.com

CONTENTS

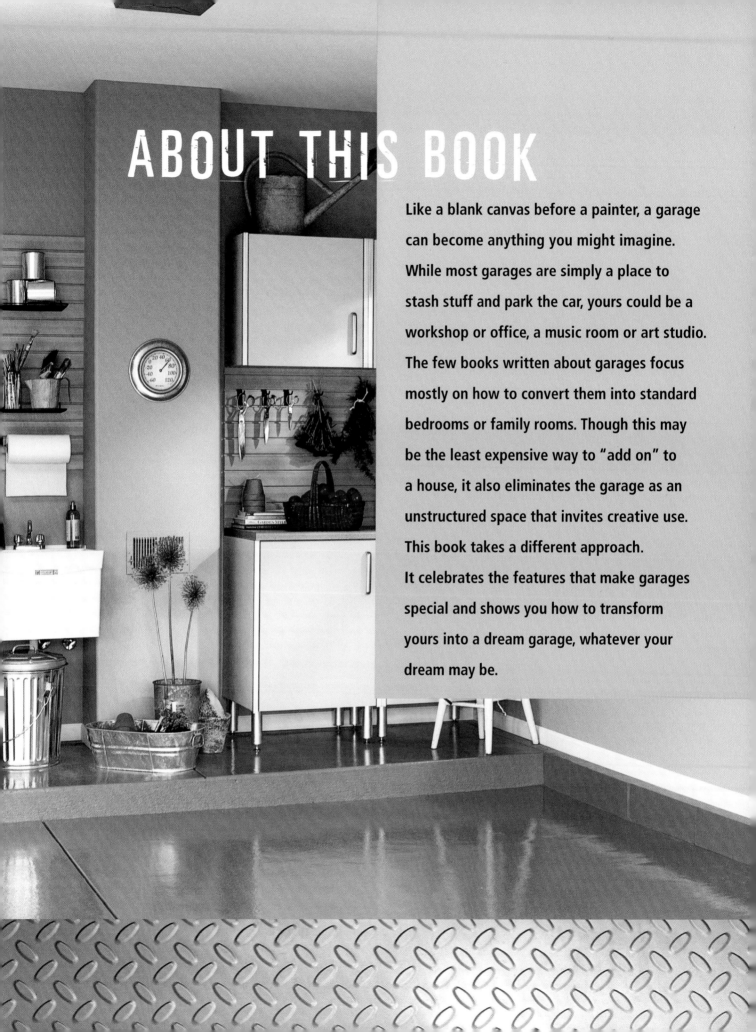

ABOUT THIS BOOK

Like a blank canvas before a painter, a garage can become anything you might imagine. While most garages are simply a place to stash stuff and park the car, yours could be a workshop or office, a music room or art studio. The few books written about garages focus mostly on how to convert them into standard bedrooms or family rooms. Though this may be the least expensive way to "add on" to a house, it also eliminates the garage as an unstructured space that invites creative use. This book takes a different approach. It celebrates the features that make garages special and shows you how to transform yours into a dream garage, whatever your dream may be.

GETTING

If your garage is full of clutter you'll need to deal with it sooner or later—especially if you plan to use the space for more than just parking the car. This chapter suggests strategies for dealing with stuff: how to sort it, how and where to get rid of it affordably and responsibly, and how to store what remains so that it's easily accessible but out of your way.

ORGANIZED

Sorting

Although cleaning out a garage can seem daunting, it can actually be enjoyable if you approach it right. Set aside a specific time and line up help if necessary. In a relatively short period, you can accomplish a tremendous change.

After a new baby, a job change, and a back injury, the family with this three-car garage had stashed so much stuff that they could not even walk through one bay. Their clean-out began with two steps that made an immediate difference: They pulled out empty boxes, and they called a charity to haul away the car buried in the middle.

Basic strategy

On the driveway or in an open area of the garage, designate spaces for three categories of stuff: items you will donate or sell, those you will keep, and those you will toss. Avoid a second round of sorting by establishing subcategories from the beginning. Create more as needed. Group items by use rather than type. For example, keep car cleaning and maintenance items together rather than create a "cleaning supplies" category with both the car sponge and the laundry detergent. Specific categories should fit your family and the way you think and live.

Start with boxes

Much of your clutter may consist of empty cardboard boxes. Label some of them to aid in sorting and then flatten the rest. Already your garage will seem less cluttered.

What to keep

Most people have no trouble sorting some items into the "donate" or "toss" piles. The problem comes in determining which things to save. Do a reality check as you sort, so that you keep only what is of real value to you.

■ If you haven't used something in a year, what is the chance that you will use it in the future? If you recall asking yourself this question during some other decluttering exercise, the answer this time around should be clear.

■ If it's broken, what is the likelihood that you will get around to fixing it?

■ Would the cost of replacing it exceed the value of the space it will occupy if you keep it?

Emotional decisions

Amid the clutter, you may encounter boxes filled with family memorabilia. Sorting these items can easily bog down your clean–out. Provided you don't have too many boxes like this, it makes more sense to label them and set them aside. You might move them into the house so you won't forget to deal with them later.

Sort only once

If you sort items into categories that are too broad, you will need to go through everything again before you can store it or get rid of it efficiently. Use the following subcategories as a start toward labeling boxes or piles within each of your main categories.

Donate or sell
- ■ To friends or relatives
- ■ To thrift shops
- ■ At a garage sale
- ■ On eBay or other Internet auction site

Toss
- ■ Garbage
- ■ Cardboard and other recyclables
- ■ Broken items

Keep
- ■ Bulk food
- ■ Household supplies
- ■ Tools
- ■ Home repair items
- ■ Car gear
- ■ Garden equipment
- ■ Sporting goods
- ■ Crafts
- ■ Holiday decorations
- ■ Future baby clothes and supplies
- ■ Memorabilia

Getting help

If cleaning out your garage seems overwhelming, get help. Professional organizers, estate-sale managers, junk-removal services, and teen employment programs are among your options.

Professional organizers

Across the country, a growing number of small businesses focus on helping people deal with clutter in homes and garages. For perhaps $50 to $75 an hour, they help with the physical work as well as the psychological aspects of sorting through piles that may bring back waves of memories. Unlike you, professional organizers don't have an emotional investment in your stuff.

They can help keep you on track. Good organizers also know who can haul away what you don't want, where to recycle unusual items, and how to outfit your garage so it stays organized.

Before you hire an organizer, spend time talking and check references. While it may be tempting to hire someone who will come in and do it all, those who insist that you stay involved

Laura Leist, left, of Eliminate Chaos, helped this homeowner reorganize her garage in just a few days using mostly existing shelving units.

will give you more long-lasting results. Organizing a garage isn't just about hauling away junk; it also involves a changed state of mind and new habits.

Organizers may recommend specific storage systems and installers. They are sometimes paid for referrals, so you

This couple brought in a professional organizing company to help deal with their garage clutter. While the pros sorted gear with an obvious purpose, these two focused on cleaning out boxes of papers and memorabilia. After five years of increasing disorganization, their garage was shipshape in just a few days.

Temporary storage

You may need to create a holding area for your piles while you set up a better storage system. If your garage still has space to park, keeping the car elsewhere for a few days is the simplest solution. Otherwise, you may get by with a tarp over items piled outside. If you're tackling a major garage remodel and have valuable items or neighborhood rules that ban tarps, consider renting a sidewalk storage box.

may want to shop around on your own as well. If you want to reuse storage systems that you already own, make your wishes clear. A good organizer may have brilliant suggestions for moving or reconfiguring them.

The National Association of Professional Organizers *(www.napo.net)* can help you contact organizers near you. Also look for advertisements in your local newspaper.

Estate-sale organizers

An estate-sale organizer may be useful if you have a garage stuffed with boxes from a relative who died or if you have marketable items—tools, sports gear, antiques—that you just want gone. Either way, an estate-sale organizer can sort, determine prices, and advertise and run your sale. In return, you'll hand over a percentage of the revenue.

If you take this approach, ask for references and call them. Check whether the organizer owns a business that sells the types of items you have. Because the organizer will determine prices, make sure they aren't set low just so the organizer can buy them for resale. Also ask what arrangements there will be for dealing with items that no one buys.

Junk-removal services

If you hire a junk-removal service, you are essentially renting a truck with a driver and crew. The crew will come in and take away whatever you ask them to haul, as long as it doesn't contain items they aren't allowed to transport (hazardous materials, for example). Do not expect the crew to make judgment calls about what is worth keeping or needs to be tossed.

Companies vary in what they charge and in how they approach their job.

Some services charge by volume or weight, from less than $100 for a couch or washing machine to hundreds for a truckload. Others charge for their time and truck, plus dump fees. If you go with one of these services and you have large quantities of furniture, metal items, or other materials that can be reused or recycled, pick a crew that works hard to divert those items to appropriate companies or agencies. If you choose a service that takes almost everything to a dump or transfer station, you may pay dump fees far higher than necessary.

Companies also vary in their policies regarding what they will or won't take. Evaluate their policies in light of what's in your garage.

Local teens

If all you need is physical help, consider hiring neighborhood teenagers. Besides saving money and getting the job done, you'll help build a sense of community. Just be sure to supervise the work so no one gets hurt.

Getting rid of junk

After you've decided what to keep, you need to get rid of the rest. While it's tempting to toss everything you don't want into the trash, cutting down on waste saves you money. You also need to deal with hazardous items responsibly.

Selling

Turn unwanted items into cash with a garage sale, through classified advertising in your local newspaper, on the Internet auction site eBay, or through a local consignment store. If you have large quantities of specialty items, such as parts for a specific model of car or old fly-fishing gear, a specialty dealer or eBay may be your best bet. A garage sale may be better if your discard pile consists mostly of general household goods and popular specialty items such as baby gear, sports equipment, and tools.

Donations

Giving your unwanted items to charity is a good thing—as long as the charity can actually use them. Charities have to pay disposal fees, just as you do. If you're not sure what a charity can use, call first. If you do donate to a non-profit, ask for a receipt if you plan to claim the value of your gift on your tax return.

Hazardous materials

Many items in your garage may qualify as hazardous materials, including paint, cleaners, oils, batteries, old fluorescent lights, and pesticides. Some communities offer ongoing disposal programs for these materials, while others set up special collection days. Learn local options by calling your city or county solid-waste disposal program. Or go to *www.earth911.org* and type in your zip code.

Recyclables

You can recycle more than bottles, cans, and newspapers. Many communities also have companies or agencies equipped to take cardboard, all types of metal, wood that's not treated with creosote or arsenic preservatives, chunks of concrete, foam, old nursery pots, batteries, and most types of plastic. To learn about your area's resources, follow the tip above.

What to do with...

Paint: Some communities collect left-over paint for graffiti-abatement programs or reformulate it for resale. Others classify oil-based paint as a hazardous product but direct homeowners to mix leftover water-based paint with clay-based kitty litter and then toss it into the trash. Check your local rules. If you can link leftover paint to a room in your house, save some for touch-ups. Save space by repackaging leftover paint when it's in a gallon can that's less than one-fourth full. Transfer it to an empty quart can, attach a label, and dab on a little paint for easy reference.

Hazardous materials: If solvents, concrete cleaners, and similar materials are still legal to sell and are still in their original containers, try to give them to someone who can use them. You might set up a freebies table at a garage sale. With pesticides, however, you may have formulas that were once legal but are now known to cause long-term harm. You must treat these as hazardous waste.

Old computers and other electronic gear: The environmental program of the Electronic Industries Alliance *(www.eiae.org)* can direct you to companies or organizations that reuse old computers, stereos, televisions, and other equipment. Through this Web site, you can also learn of programs that recycle the components of obsolete or broken equipment.

Appliances: If a stove, refrigerator, or other appliance is relatively new and working, you can probably sell it through classified advertising or at a garage sale. Or you may be able to give it to a charity, but call first. Many charities do not accept these heavy, bulky items. If the appliance is broken, you will probably need to dispose of it. Call your city or county solid-waste office or your local trash company.

Old clothing: Don't expect to sell lots of old clothing at a garage sale. People interested in this type of bargain are more likely to shop at resale stores with dressing rooms. Thrift stores need clothing that can go directly onto the racks for sale or be bundled for shipment to poorer countries. If you have clothing that's too far gone, phone local charities and ask whether they can recycle them as rags or fiber. Do not burden charities that toss this clothing and pay to have it hauled away.

Baby gear: Thrift stores generally welcome baby gear, and it moves fast at garage sales. However, certain models of strollers and car seats have been recalled by the Consumer Product Safety Commission and no reputable store wants to sell them. To avoid having to keep up with the specifics, some thrift stores turn down all models. Consignment shops that specialize in children's items are more likely to accept seats and strollers that are still fine. You may also pass on safe equipment by selling it at a garage sale or giving it to a friend or relative.

Building materials: Usable materials, ranging from long 2 by 4s to that old kitchen sink, should not be set out with the trash except as a last resort. Try selling them at a garage sale or through classified advertising. Or take them to a used building materials store in your area. For locations, look in your phone book under "building materials—used" or contact the Used Building Materials Association

(www.ubma.org). You can also post a "free" sign on them in front of your house.

Craft items: Thrift shops may welcome these, or you can try selling them at garage sales or through classified advertising. In many communities, nonprofit organizations or even individual artists accept these, often to use for activities with kids. Check with your community's solid-waste coordinator or arts center.

13

Storing what you keep

Once you've sorted your stuff, you need to put back what you keep. On the following pages, you'll see a wide array of garages with storage systems that work. In some, every part goes back to a specific place. In others, items are stored in loosely arranged zones.

In any garage, the state of key areas determines whether the entire space seems cluttered or neat. If some things will inevitably be left out of place in your newly organized garage, define areas that must be left clear. Upholsterer Carolyn Brown uses a carpet, which doubles as a space where she assembles futons. Around the carpet, but never on it, she stores boxes of padding, bolts of fabric, and tools of her trade.

Basic Strategies

1. Store like things together. Organize by activity, not type of item. If you use paper plates only for picnics, house your extras with picnic gear, not holiday supplies or paper supplies. Create kits stocked with everything you need for specific activities.

2. Keep things visible. If you can't see it, you may forget you have it. You'll wind up buying another bottle of windshield-washer solution when you already have three opened jugs.

3. Make prime use of real estate. Shelves that are very high or very low are harder to use than those at eye level. Store your most used items where you can reach them easily.

4. Minimize horizontal surfaces, especially near doors. They inevitably collect clutter because they make it easier to set something down than to put it away.

5. Minimize needless tidying. If you find yourself repeatedly taking out specific objects that then become clutter because you haven't put them back, try to set up a storage system that lets these items stay out yet organized. For example, if your work-

bench always fills with tools that weren't returned after projects in the house, store the tools in a caddy. Or invest in a second set of tools to use in the house.

6. Don't crowd storage areas. Leave enough space so you can move items in and out and add new gear.

Storage boxes

Clear plastic boxes with tight-fitting lids are great for storing groups of things, such as picnic supplies and holiday decorations. The plastic lets you see what's inside, and it keeps out rodents. It may also block moisture from moving in or out, which could be good or bad. Humid weather and wide temperature swings may cause con-

Cabinets with adjustable shelves keep this garage organized even with containers of many sizes and styles.

densation within the boxes, and the plastic will keep the moisture from evaporating. That, in turn, may allow mold to grow on the contents. Protect against this by adding silica gel or another drying agent to the boxes.

Types of plastic

For casual storage, any type of plastic will do. But for long-term storage of heirloom fabrics, important papers, and other keepsakes, use boxes made of polypropylene. Look for the number 5 in the plastic recycling symbol. Rubbermaid and Sterilite use this inert type of plastic, as do companies that cater to

professional conservators. Some other plastics degrade over time, releasing chemicals that cause irreversible damage to some items. Consider storing family treasures inside the house instead.

Sizes

If you do invest in plastic boxes, buy several sizes that are multiples of one another. When two small boxes take up the same shelf space as one large one, for example, it's easier to use shelf space efficiently. Sticking to sizes that combine evenly also allows you to modify your storage system as your possessions change, without launching a full-scale reorganization. Generally, if you stick to one brand, you'll automatically wind up with complementary sizes.

Hiding it all

A movable garage system makes sense for families who relocate often. Chuck and Erin Bresnahan chose Gladiator GarageWorks for this reason, and because everything can be stored neatly behind matching doors. The specific design is unique to this brand, but the concept is similar to that behind other systems. Storage accessories hang from slotted panels. Once a panel has been screwed into wall studs, hanging or repositioning takes just a few minutes. And when you move, the accessories can go with you.

Baskets, cabinets, and tubs

The Bresnahans use a variety of storage methods, depending on the size of objects and how they're used. Wire baskets keep balls where they're quick to grab and easy to put back. Closed cabinets hold household items. Seasonal sports gear stows away in plastic tubs on the floor.

Shoe rack

Perfect for airing out shoes, wire racks clip onto the slotted wall panels that are the heart of this storage system. A wide variety of accessories are available for some systems, but they are not necessarily interchangeable from one system to the next. Gladiator, for example, spaces slots $2\frac{3}{8}$ inches apart, while 3-inch spacing is common with other brands.

Added floor space

The Bresnahan home has wide garage doors facing the street. When the cars are out and the doors are open, everyone can see how they store their stuff. Thanks to the family's hide-it-all storage system, the main expanse usually stays neat. Neighborhood children were quick to recognize the opportunities: The Bresnahan garage often becomes their play space.

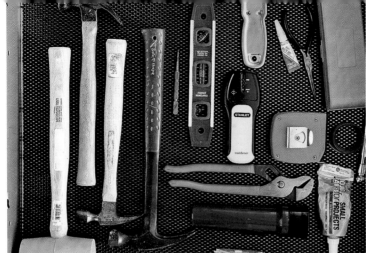

Padded drawers

The Bresnahans lined their tool drawers with soft pads to prevent the screech of metal scraping against metal. You could also cut up the type of rubber mats that keeps area rugs from slipping.

Lockers

Each girl gets her own locker for sports gear, a setup that keeps smelly shin guards and athletic shoes out of bedrooms. When it's time to clean the garage, the lockers roll away from the wall easily because they sit on locking casters. Over the cabinets, two shelves hang from slotted panels.

A compact workshop

Three upper cabinets, two lower sets of drawers, and a slab of butcher-block maple on legs give the family a well-organized place to tackle home repair projects. A shop vacuum conveniently fits between the drawer units.

Extra refrigeration

This line of garage gear includes a combination refrigerator-freezer. The bottom two-thirds of this appliance is a dedicated freezer, while the top third switches to be either a refrigerator or a freezer. Other features include locking casters and a built-in heater to keep beverages from freezing if the garage temperature drops too low. But a refrigerator designed for a garage isn't your only option. You may want to shop for an Energy Star–rated refrigerator or a dedicated freezer and set it on a base with locking casters. People often move old kitchen refrigerators to the garage as spares, but the old appliances typically waste energy.

Bicycle storage

In this three-car garage, the family opted to devote most of one bay to bicycle storage. At a sporting goods store, they bought a floor rack, which steadies one wheel of each bike. This is the easiest type of bike storage system to use.

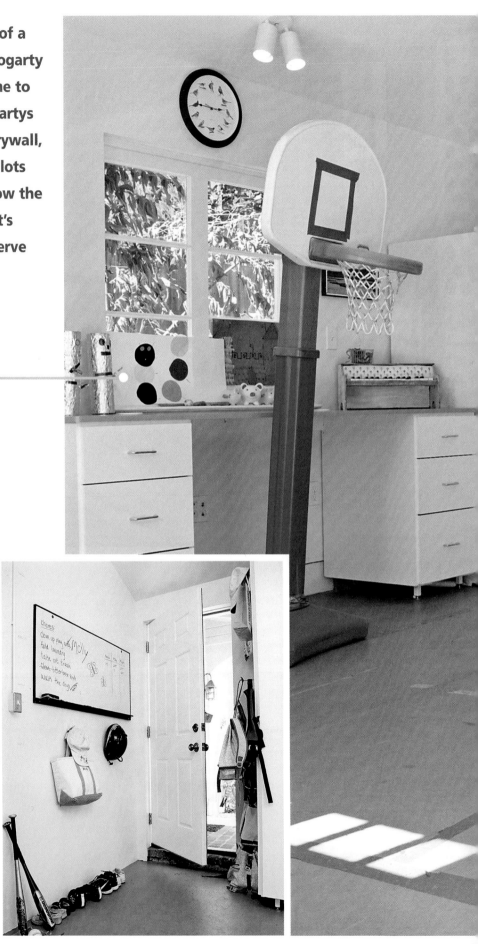

he day a rat jumped out of a laundry basket, Megan Fogarty decided it was finally time to renovate the garage. The Fogartys closed up the framing with drywall, added windows, and created lots of enclosed storage space. Now the garage has a neat look, and it's clean and bright enough to serve as a play area too.

Homework center

When the children get older, they can do their homework at this desk along one sidewall. Planning ahead, the Fogartys wired an Internet connection to this area before they closed in the walls. Craft materials and tools are hidden away in six deep drawers.

Mudroom

Backpacks, boots, and other gear no longer clutter the front entrance to the house. The equipment now belongs on hooks that flank a side door in the garage. Although the space is barely more than a hallway, it functions like a mudroom.

Overhead cubbies

Instead of stashing boxes on ceiling joists, the Fogartys built storage areas into the ceiling. The cubbies, enclosed except on one side, store bulky items that the family uses for camping trips and other occasional activities.

Ball time

Now that the garage is bright and clean, it has become a play space. The Fogartys plan to carpet the garage eventually, though not until their kids have graduated to larger basketball courts. In the meantime, the family patched and painted the concrete floor so it's cheerier and easier to clean.

Sliding door

The Fogartys opted for a sliding garage door so that the ceiling would stay clear for their children's basketball games. Glass panels along the top of the doors give the garage a friendly cottage look, and they help bring light into a space that used to seem dark. Below the glass, the doors give the kids a place to display their art.

Large items

Another cubby over the door provides space for fishing poles and other items too awkward or bulky to store elsewhere. Megan uses a ladder for access, but it would also be possible to install pull-down attic stairs.

Cabinet wall

Past the mudroom area, the garage now has a series of four cabinets, all on adjustable legs so they're level and off the concrete. Cleaning supplies go in one area, while toys and craft items belong in another.

Laundry area

The washer and dryer are still in the garage, but the laundry area is clean and tidy now. Open shelves below the two upper cabinets store detergent and other essentials within easy reach. Downlights illuminate the area.

Artist at work

Although the desk area will eventually become a homework center, it now functions more as a place to do crafts.

When designing the garage under their hillside home, Eddie and Sherri Lourenco had a few key storage issues to consider. They needed to store a boat and vehicles as well as general household gear. Their architect figured out how to get the boat in, and the Lourencos found clever solutions for other storage needs.

Post planning

For structural reasons, the garage needed a support post in the middle. Thin posts can be a hazard because people may not notice them until it's too late. So the Lourencos beefed up the post, added baseboard trim, and treated it like a mini wall. They placed a cabinet and chop saw on one side.

Extra bathroom
A few steps from the garage is a bathroom. For someone working in the garage, it's far more convenient than the ones in the living quarters.

Ventilation
Because the garage sits underneath only part of the house, the Lourencos had to be careful not to cut off air circulation in the remaining crawl space. They created an attractive, functional airway by framing the opening as if it were a series of small windows. They covered the area with mesh.

Workshop area
The Lourencos used their old kitchen cabinets to create a workshop area along a sidewall at the back of the garage. They were short a few pieces for the arrangement they wanted, so they tracked down a few new pieces of the same brand.

Storage cabinets

Using materials from home centers, the Lourencos built spacious storage cabinets that keep everything out of sight yet open wide when necessary. First they installed 2-foot-deep wire shelves along two walls of their workshop area. In front of those, they installed floor-to-ceiling sliding doors. They can slide all doors to one side if they have something especially bulky to stash or if they want to reorganize. But if they just need to grab a cooler and head to the lake, they can open a single door.

Boat parking

The Lourencos built their garage with a sloped ceiling so that their 25-foot Cobalt boat would fit inside. The architect miscalculated on the space needed for Eddie's work truck, however, so he has to park it outside. Lesson: Triple-check key measurements.

Kid zone

The Lourencos' young son uses the garage mostly to play ball with his parents. Their smooth, clean terrazzo floor can eventually be used for tricycle riding and other activities.

Workshop extras

The shop area includes many details that add to the pleasure of working there. It includes a sink with hot and cold water, as well as an under-counter refrigerator. Tools are neatly organized either in the cabinets or on the pegboard wall. On the overhead shelf sits a boom box.

The organizing principle of this garage was clear: to create a space where it would be fun to work on vintage motorcycles yet still preserve the garage as a parking area for two automobiles. Calling in Cabinet Concepts, a company that specializes in custom garage cabinetry, was the first step.

Vise detail

To accommodate the handle of the woodworking vise, the cabinet company did a little fancy trimming on the drawer front underneath. The countertop edge is built like the top of a traditional woodworker's bench, so it's equipped for bench dogs. These holdfasts fit into slots created with two 1-inch-thick pieces of hardwood sandwiched on either side of shorter pieces spaced about ¾ inches apart.

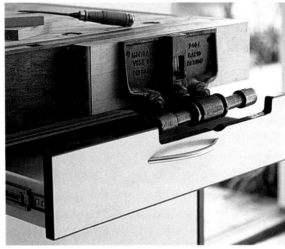

Spacious work area

Cabinets along one sidewall store tools and supplies. The long countertop gives the owner plenty of space to lay out motorcycle parts. A machinist vise is at one end, mounted on a section of countertop that's covered with stainless steel. The woodworking vise is at the other end, where a plywood top protects chisel tips from becoming dull if they're set down carelessly.

Doors that fit

One wide door and one narrow one help make a pantry-style closet as useful as possible. The narrow door's dimensions were established first. The width is the maximum that allows the door to open fully without blocking the big garage door. The other door's width matches the remaining space available for the cabinet.

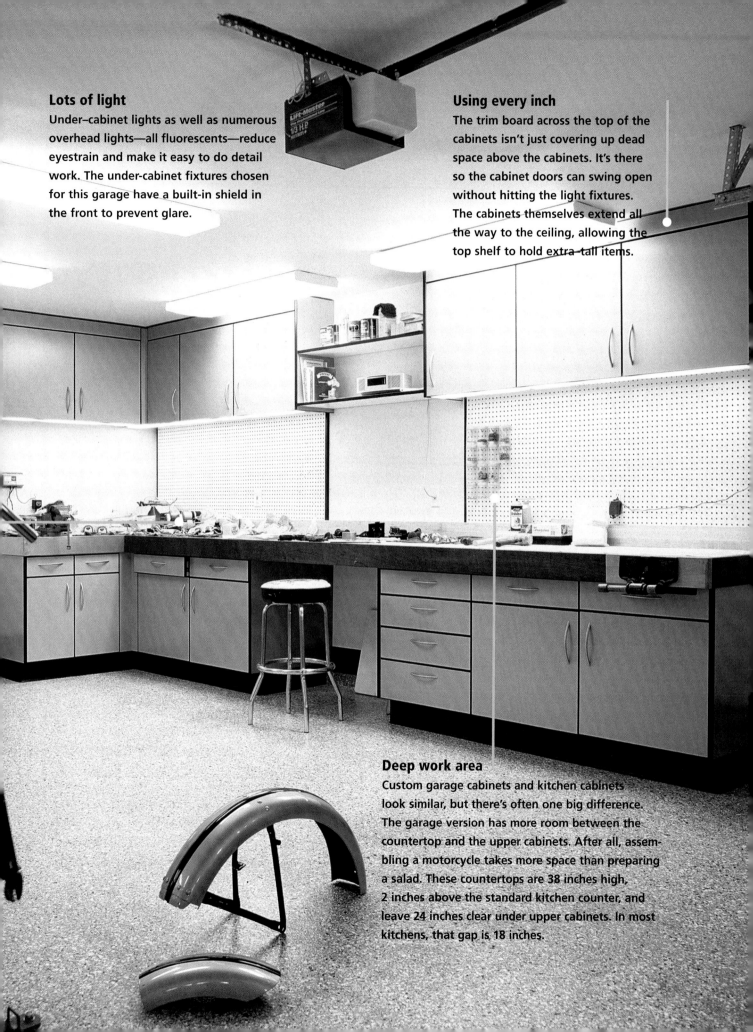

Lots of light

Under–cabinet lights as well as numerous overhead lights—all fluorescents—reduce eyestrain and make it easy to do detail work. The under-cabinet fixtures chosen for this garage have a built-in shield in the front to prevent glare.

Using every inch

The trim board across the top of the cabinets isn't just covering up dead space above the cabinets. It's there so the cabinet doors can swing open without hitting the light fixtures. The cabinets themselves extend all the way to the ceiling, allowing the top shelf to hold extra-tall items.

Deep work area

Custom garage cabinets and kitchen cabinets look similar, but there's often one big difference. The garage version has more room between the countertop and the upper cabinets. After all, assembling a motorcycle takes more space than preparing a salad. These countertops are 38 inches high, 2 inches above the standard kitchen counter, and leave 24 inches clear under upper cabinets. In most kitchens, that gap is 18 inches.

With each tool, its parts
Beyl stores each major tool and its accessories close together. His routers sit on a shelf below a sliding door that holds router bits. Under the routers are pull-out drawers with additional router gear.

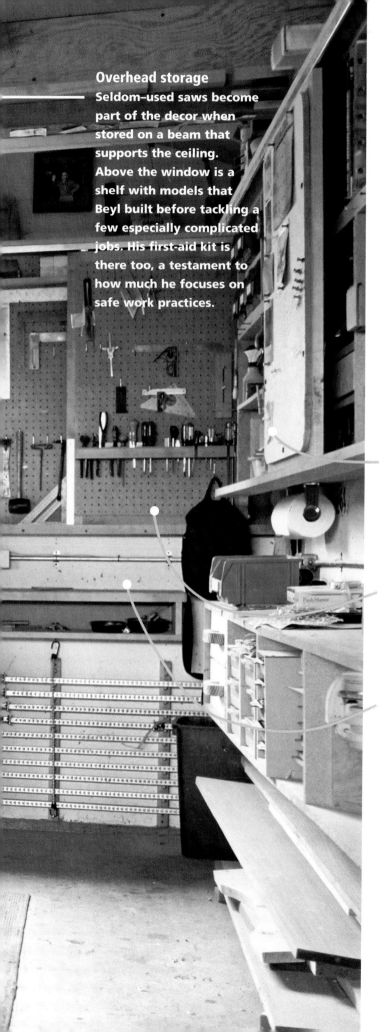

Overhead storage
Seldom–used saws become part of the decor when stored on a beam that supports the ceiling. Above the window is a shelf with models that Beyl built before tackling a few especially complicated jobs. His first-aid kit is there too, a testament to how much he focuses on safe work practices.

Keeping it all visible

When David Beyl set out to create an efficient woodworking shop in his two-car garage, he wanted all his key tools within sight and reach. He placed his workbench in the center of an 8-foot-deep bump-out at the back of the garage and lined nearby walls with tool storage—a good strategy for anyone with lots of tools or supplies.

A place for notes

For a shop bulletin board, Beyl covered one of the sliding doors with a scrap of Homasote. Made mostly from re-cycled newspapers, this inexpensive material insulates and blocks noise, so Beyl also used it to line the walls. The material comes in 4-by-8-foot sheets.

Double-layer shelves

Instead of standard doors, most upper cabinets have sliding doors covered with pegboard and narrow shelves. This nearly doubles Beyl's wall display space, allowing him to see the tools he needs so he doesn't have to search.

The right height

To increase his work surface without cutting into storage space, Beyl built base cabinets the same height as his work-bench. This allows him to use all the surfaces to support long pieces of wood.

Pegboard plus

To create two-layer storage on his garage walls, Beyl used pegboard *(below)*, an inexpensive material sold at home centers and lumberyards. He installed standard hooks and homemade racks to store router bits, chisels, and other tools.

Double-duty drawers

Beyl often teaches woodworking classes away from his shop, so he designed pullout drawers that double as tool caddies *(above)*. When he heads out to class, he grabs a router and a drawer stocked with its accessories. When he returns, he slips the drawer back in.

Numbered boxes

Miscellaneous parts and supplies go into numbered cardboard boxes. Clipped to a cupboard nearby is Beyl's handwritten log of the contents. He stores most boxes off the floor so his shop is easier to clean.

Rolling cart

To store plywood scraps, Beyl built a rolling bin *(below)* that solves several problems. The cart has a high back and partially open sides, which keep the plywood straight while still allowing him easy access. He wheels the cart out when he wants a piece and then rolls it back under the lumber rack so his wife's car fits alongside.

Lumber

Lumber *(above)* is difficult to store properly because of its weight and tendency to warp if not fully supported. Most heavy-duty shelving systems use triangular braces, which get in the way when you're trying to store long pieces. Beyl's solution was to drill a series of ⅞-inch-diameter holes in 2 by 4s that he attached to the wall by first inserting ledger boards at the back of the 2 by 4s and then screwing the ledgers to studs. Short lengths of pipe fit snugly in the holes, creating strong, obstruction-free supports for lumber. Plywood shelves rest on the pipes in some areas, allowing Beyl to store small pieces of wood.

Clamps

Beyl rests his bar clamps and some of his spring clamps on dowels. Other clamps fit over a thin horizontal piece of wood. The entire collection stays within easy reach.

Suzy West runs a scrapbooking business in her two-car garage, so she needs to store thousands of kinds of paper, ribbon, stickers, and other decorative bits. The items must be out where her customers can see them.

Door space

To keep supplies visible, West needs a lot of display space. But the back wall of the garage is devoted to the family laundry and the sidewalls aren't big enough to show off everything. So West reclaimed the wall occupied by the garage door. She set up side-by-side wire shelving units, 21 in all, across the space. Because they are freestanding and lightweight, West can easily move them when she needs to open the big garage door to load up the car for scrapbooking shows.

Flexible seating and work space

Lightweight folding tables and plastic stacking chairs create a work space that expands or contracts to fit the number of customers who show up each day. West stores nothing on the tables, as they fill up fast with her customers' supplies.

Rolling carts

West stocks rolling carts with hole punches, scissors, and other tools she supplies for her customers. When customers need something, they just pull a cart close and everything is within easy reach. Yet when it's time to clean up, all the tools go back into their proper places quickly.

Fabric ceiling
Although most of West's garage is devoted to scrapbooking, she still finds space for family storage and laundry. She stashes boxes above the ceiling joists and along the back wall, where she also has a washer and dryer. She tacked up lengths of inexpensive fabric to hide these areas.

Pegboard

To display lightweight items, West uses pegboard and a variety of slip-on hooks. Her hooks have ball ends, which are safer than blunt tips. The balls also help keep items from coming off accidentally.

Wire racks

For displaying hundreds of kinds of paper, West found the best solution at a company that sells fixtures to craft-supply stores. She bought wire racks that allow customers to see their options and remove individual sheets without wrinkling them.

For ways to display or store other problematic materials, try visiting retail stores that focus on the same items and note what storage systems they use. Then check the phone book under "store fixtures" or "store fixtures—used," or turn to the Web.

Bar coding

West has the ultimate solution for keeping track of her supplies: She bar-codes everything. Customers walk around her garage and collect decorative materials for their projects. Then they sit down at her computer (at the back of the garage), log on to individual accounts, and scan their items. The computer program adds sales tax, and West's printer spews out invoices. Scanning equipment costs only a few hundred dollars, but creating a database to link the codes with other information might cost several thousand.

Bins

One of West's favorite storage units has wooden shelves and plastic bins tilted to keep the contents visible. The bins pull out so that customers can remove whole collections of buttons, eyelets, and other items to inspect them more closely. West found this unit at a department store, where it was being marketed for toy storage. Companies that sell store fixtures offer a wide selection of similar units with bins made of plastic or heavy-duty cardboard. Store fixtures also tend to be available in wider and deeper dimensions.

Zone approach in a small garage

Jerry Toner lives in an early 1900s Craftsman bungalow in a neighborhood filled with houses of similar vintage. When he set out to build a garage, he wanted it to look similar to the modest one-car structures that were typical when the neighborhood was new. However, he had to fit in a lot more stuff than people did then. He makes it work by clustering his tools and supplies.

Small-projects zone

Light streaming in from two generously sized windows illuminates a 2-foot-deep countertop that Toner built along one sidewall. He does small projects here, using screws and nails stored at eye level. This counter also doubles as a stand for his chop saw. The other sidewall, just out of view, has a lower countertop. Toner uses it to store bulky pieces, such as kitchen cabinets, until he's ready to take them to houses he's remodeling. He's found that his shop can hold only about half the cabinets he needs for a good-sized kitchen, so he tackles large jobs in stages.

Central work zone

Toner's 16-by-20-foot garage is dominated by a worktable at the center. He assembles most of his cabinets and other large projects here, so the surrounding storage is designed to keep tools and supplies within easy reach. The 4-by-8-foot table, made from a full sheet of plywood, doubles as an outfeed support for Toner's table saw. The garage is just long enough that he can rip a sheet of plywood when the door is down.

Loading zone

Because Toner does most of his work in the houses he remodels, he has a large collection of portable tools. He stores them on open shelves next to the main garage door so that he can back his truck in and load up with no wasted steps. Toner lives in Seattle, and this setup allows him to keep his tools dry when he loads and unloads in the rain.

Assembly zone

Whether Toner is gluing or nailing his projects, the tools he needs are just a step away. He hooks bar and C-clamps over a piece of wood molded with a lip. Spring clamps, attached to one another, hang from a hook. The coiled yellow hose connects to a pipe that leads to Toner's air compressor, which powers his finish nailer and other tools.

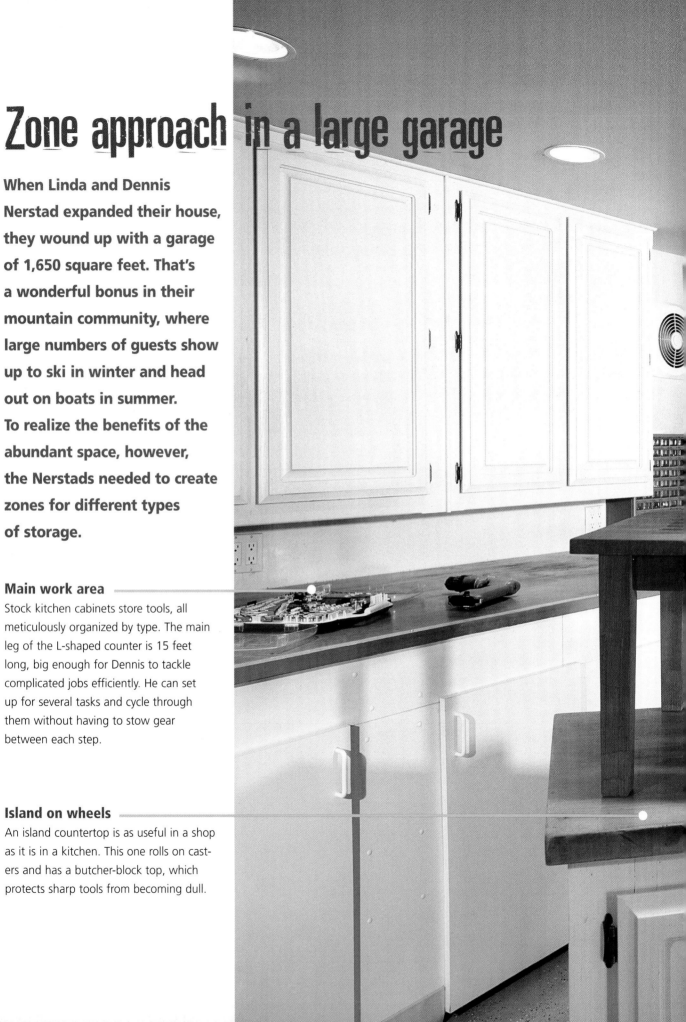

Zone approach in a large garage

When Linda and Dennis Nerstad expanded their house, they wound up with a garage of 1,650 square feet. That's a wonderful bonus in their mountain community, where large numbers of guests show up to ski in winter and head out on boats in summer. To realize the benefits of the abundant space, however, the Nerstads needed to create zones for different types of storage.

Main work area

Stock kitchen cabinets store tools, all meticulously organized by type. The main leg of the L-shaped counter is 15 feet long, big enough for Dennis to tackle complicated jobs efficiently. He can set up for several tasks and cycle through them without having to stow gear between each step.

Island on wheels

An island countertop is as useful in a shop as it is in a kitchen. This one rolls on casters and has a butcher-block top, which protects sharp tools from becoming dull.

Game time
Dennis can work on his home maintenance chores while he listens to the radio or keeps up with a ballgame on TV. Equipment in this area also includes an exhaust fan and a weather monitor.

Metalworking area
A granite slab, left over from when the Nerstads remodeled their kitchen, fits into the counter in the metalworking area. The stone provides a heat-resistant, fireproof surface for welding and soldering. It also stands up to sparks from the grinder.

Garage zone

The Nerstads have about 780 square feet in their "garage zone," the space at the front where they park three vehicles. They organized this area so it's easy to keep tidy. The community gets 15 feet of snow in a typical year, so the Nerstads plumbed drains into the floor under each parking spot. That way, accumulated snow on the vehicles can simply melt off in the garage without causing a flood. They also installed a tap with hot and cold water so they can wash vehicles indoors when necessary. A rolling cart holds tools and supplies.

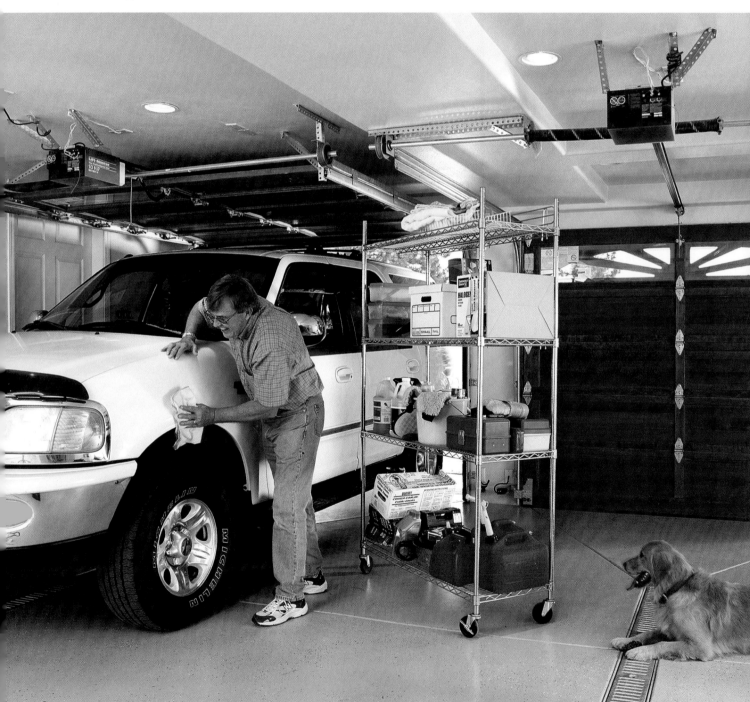

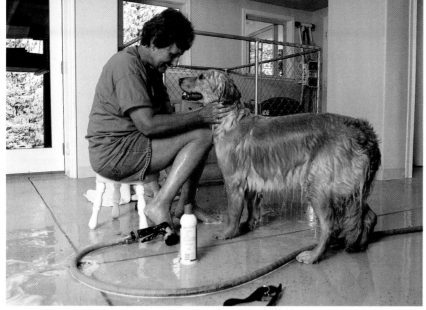

Dog zone

One bay of the Nerstads' garage is extra long, providing space for the workshop and a fourth parking area. The Nerstads don't have four cars, so they use that space for Nugget, their golden retriever. They shampoo her here, using the nearby water supply. When the job is done, they squeegee the suds down the floor drain. The Nerstads also created a 6-by-6-foot kennel for Nugget. The metal fencing allows the dog to stay close to Dennis when he's in the shop, without risk of tipping over a can of paint or picking up a metal sliver. Next to the kennel, the Nerstads store bulk dog food.

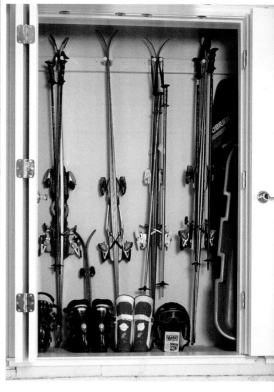

Storage zones

The Nerstads created several storage zones. In a narrow space alongside one parking spot, they built a closet with two sets of bifold doors. One set opens to reveal a rack that holds 5 pairs of skis, while the other conceals boating supplies. The main storage area is a room about 15 by 15 feet next to the workshop. It has plenty of room for luggage, bulk food, and miscellaneous items.

Interior door

An interior roll-up door separates the garage area from the shop. The Nerstads lower this door when they want to isolate the workshop—to confine sawdust to that space, for instance. The door, a standard one-car-garage model, is wide enough that Dennis can bring a vehicle into the shop area if he wishes.

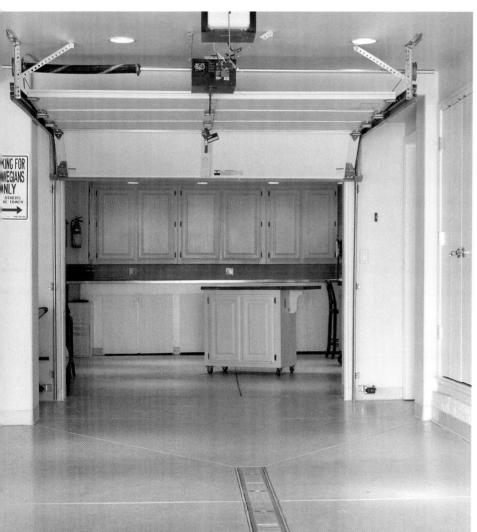

Setting up a storage system

As you rethink the way you use your garage, you may wonder whether to invest in a full-scale storage system. A single system creates the cleanest look, but it comes at a price: typically $5,000 to $10,000 and possibly much more. Before you decide, you may want to consider the following issues.

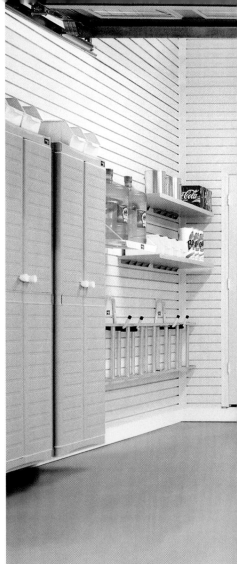

Capacity

Look at marketing brochures with a skeptical eye. Do they show garages that look neat mostly because so few items are in them? Compare what you need to store with the space various systems offer. Consider not only what's in your garage now, especially if you just cleaned it, but what it's likely to hold over time. If you need to add a lot more shelves, wire baskets, and other accessories to the basic package, it could boost the cost significantly.

Dimensions

Be sure to consider width, height, and depth. Look for adjustable shelves and ones that aren't too shallow to be useful. Base cabinets can be 24 inches deep, especially if you have a work-bench top, while upper cabinets may be more accessible if they are shallower. Uppers 12 inches deep keep everything within view; ones 16 inches deep store a lot more. Floor-to-ceiling cabinets are typically up to 24 inches deep. If you plan to store gear in clear plastic boxes, consider their size when you select a storage system. You probably don't want shelves that hold 2½ boxes.

Accessories

A special hook for storing a wheelbarrow, a wire basket for balls, a storage rack designed especially for a skateboard—these are the fun details of garage storage. Don't pick a storage system on the basis of its accessories, however. The amount and configuration of the storage and the quality of key components are far more important. You can always buy accessories separately.

A company that specializes in custom garage cabinets built this 24-foot-long storage wall and workbench for about $10,000. The cabinets are made of plywood coated with high-pressure laminate that looks like pear wood. Good custom designs make every inch count. With a set of cabinets similar to this, even a one-car garage can have more storage and work space than many far larger spaces have.

ABOVE: The company that makes this storage system finds that customers typically spend $4,000 to $6,000 for wall panels and accessories they think they'll need. Later, they order more cabinets and shelves to store big, bulky items.

Simple shelves supported by brackets that clip into standards keep everything in sight. Before you buy a system of this type, consider whether it allows some shelving to be deeper than the rest. The setup alongside the car costs approximately $600.

Overhead shelves are ideal for bulky but relatively light-weight items, such as sleeping bags, that you don't use often. Books would be too heavy. The system shown above, including the ladder brackets, starts at around $100 for a 36-inch-wide section.

Cabinets

For enclosed storage with lots of space, cabinets similar to those found in kitchens or pantries are your best bet. They feature adjustable shelves, sturdy drawer slides, and a combination of upper and lower cabinets. Buy units in kits or order them from companies that specialize in garage or kitchen storage.

Materials

Most garage cabinets are made of particleboard or plywood, but metal and plastic are also options. Standard particleboard costs least but isn't as strong or smooth as the industrial particleboard used by some cabinet companies. Medium-density fiberboard (MDF) is even stronger. The biggest drawback to any type of particleboard is that it might swell if it gets wet, which can ruin the cabinet. Plywood is stronger and fares better if it gets wet. Metal rusts if the paint seal fails. With plastic, the big issue is the weight limit, which is often lower than with other materials.

Coatings

Although you can buy bare or painted cabinets, most of those made from wood or wood fibers are coated with thin plastic, either melamine or a high-pressure laminate. Laminate costs more, but it's thicker, tougher, and more resistant to moisture. It also adds stiffness. Particleboard shelves coated with high-pressure laminate can carry three times as much weight without sagging than bare or melamine-coated particleboard. And high-pressure laminate comes in hundreds of shades and patterns, while melamine is available in just a few colors. Most metal cabinets are painted. Plastic cabinets don't need a protective coating.

Supports

Most garage floors slope so that water can drain out. Rather than level every cabinet, many storage companies mount components to walls. This makes it easier for you to clean the garage, and it reduces the chance that the cabinets will wick water off the floor. The trade-off is that wall-mounted systems have weight limits, so evaluate them based on what you will store.

BELOW: Garage cabinets can be both stylish and functional. This 22-foot-long custom setup, which cost about $8,500, provides deep drawers, lots of shelf space, and two work surfaces (butcher-block maple and stainless steel). But what sets it apart is the appearance: bright colors, under-counter lights, and bar pulls that echo the look of a mechanic's tool chest. The cabinets are plywood coated with high-pressure laminate.

ABOVE: To prevent tall, deep cabinets from sagging over time, some companies rest them on the floor. You can do this and still get the moisture protection and ease of cleaning that wall-mounted cabinets offer. The manufacturer of the $2,500 system shown above elevates the pieces on height-adjustable legs. Cabinet levelers and casters also work. These cabinets are made of particleboard coated with high-pressure laminate.

You can also buy metal cabinets. This $3,000 arrangement combines steel pegboard, a hardwood workbench top, and steel cabinets made by a company specializing in industrial workstations and storage systems. The drawers glide on steel rollers and carry hundreds of pounds. A four-drawer parts cabinet under the work surface comes stocked with fasteners and fittings.

Shelves

Shelves can hide behind doors or stay out in the open. Either way, they'll probably provide much of your garage storage. Following are some things you can do to keep them from sagging.

Strength

Shelf standards with two rows of holes *(below)* support approximately twice the weight of single-track standards. They also hold brackets more securely. To speed installation, some manufacturers suggest installing a top rail and then hanging shelf standards from it. This is fine for light loads, up to 75 pounds per foot of top track. But in a garage, shelves tend to collect lots of stuff. Prevent problems by screwing standards to studs. Installed that way, the same system holds up to 600 pounds per standard.

ABOVE : Though these wooden brackets are thin and lightweight, they carry heavy loads, provided they are screwed into studs, not just drywall.

BELOW: Some shelving systems allow you to incorporate special features such as hooks for tools, hoses, and ladders.

Strategies

To keep shelves from sagging, try these ideas:

■ Store less stuff.

■ Provide enough support. With ¾-inch particleboard, don't span more than 19 inches if you expect to store heavy things, such as boxes filled with papers. MDF shelves of the same thickness can go 21 inches. With pine boards or plywood, the distance stretches to 33 or 34 inches.

■ To bolster a wood shelf, glue and screw a piece of hardwood (perhaps 1 by 2 inches) to the front. Supporting the back also helps, if your shelf design allows it.

■ With wire shelving, get the type with little triangles of reinforcement along the edges (above) if you want long spans that can handle heavy loads. Use standard wire shelving with straight bars for light loads or short spans.

ABOVE: Support posts at all corners help this type of shelving handle heavier loads than shelving that's supported only from the back. The edge reinforcing also adds strength. RIGHT: Sagging shelves look unsightly but still hold stuff—until fasteners eventually give way.

Drawers

Drawers are as useful in your garage as they are in your kitchen. Just make sure they are extra sturdy if you use them to store power tools or other heavy items. Besides standard drawers, you may want to consider some special types for your garage.

Trash drawer

When there's trash to toss in this garage, it goes through the swinging door and drops into a can concealed inside the cabinet. When the can is full, it slides out on a base, a feature borrowed from kitchen cabinet designs.

Deep drawers

Extra-deep, extra-wide drawers come in handy for all sorts of things. When the custom cabinet shown above was designed, the drawer was intended to store a long vacuum hose for cleaning out the cars and garage. But the drawer was claimed for another use: storing bicycle helmets and balls.

Bins

When you need more drawers than your cabinets will hold, consider adding bins. You can buy free-standing bins, bins that stack, and bins arranged in cases. Whatever the size or style, a tilted front opening lets you see inside. It also allows you to reach right in without opening doors or drawers.

■ Create a recycling center with jumbo-size stacking bins.

■ Stash hats, mittens, and umbrellas in bins by the door to the house.

Heavy-duty drawers

These drawers *(above)* look ordinary enough, but their heavy-duty hardware makes them more functional. Each set of glides handles 90 pounds, so the drawers can hold wrenches, hammers, and other weighty tools and still open and close smoothly. The glides are the full-extension type, which means you can see into the very back of the drawers. And they have a "positive close" feature, which lets them snug into place on their own once someone closes them most of the way.

Desk drawers

The ergonomics of computer use have made classic office desks nearly obsolete, but their super-sturdy drawers still provide great storage. Below, heavy metalworking tools are kept in an old desk.

Slotwall systems

A growing number of companies now offer systems in which shelves, baskets, hooks, and even cabinets hang from grooved panels attached to walls. Similar panels, known as "slotwall" or "slatwall," have been used in store displays for decades. Once you install the panels, you can easily add or rearrange the accessories. Everything looks coordinated, and it's all off the floor.

Panel types

Most garage systems use panels made of PVC or CVPC, a related plastic. Most store displays use panels made of MDF, a wood–fiber product. The plastics aren't damaged by water or insects, as MDF can be, but MDF costs less. You may want to evaluate how likely water damage might be in your garage. Companies that sell plastic panels warn that high humidity can compromise the strength of MDF, but stores in all areas of the country have used it successfully for years.

Dimensions

The MDF panels come in 4-by-8-foot sheets weighing about 100 pounds. The plastic panels are sold in strips, often 12 or 15 inches wide by 8 or 10 feet long, making them easier to handle. Whatever the material, for the widest choice in accessories, chose panels with 3 inches between grooves, the standard for store displays.

Strength

MDF slotwall holds about 35 pounds per 6-inch-long bracket (or half that per 12-inch-long bracket, because of the lever effect). The weight limit is fine if you're storing miscellaneous sports gear on hooks, but it's not enough to support cabinets. For that, you need plastic panels or MDF panels with aluminum inserts in the grooves. Either option is about twice as strong as plain MDF.

ABOVE: A wide variety of hooks and other accessories are available for slotted panels, so you should be able to devise a way to store things that you use most often, such as a tire pump.

BELOW: To install slotwall, screw through the grooves into wall studs. Some plastic slotwall comes with hidden fasteners. If you use these, no screws will show on your completed wall.

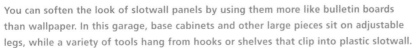

You can soften the look of slotwall panels by using them more like bulletin boards than wallpaper. In this garage, base cabinets and other large pieces sit on adjustable legs, while a variety of tools hang from hooks or shelves that clip into plastic slotwall.

Metal grid systems

Metal grids are another great storage solution borrowed from store displays. Grids are attractive and very sturdy, so you can really load them up with baskets, hooks, and other accessories.

Beefy grids

The strongest grids consist of ¼-inch-thick bars welded where they cross. They carry a lot of weight, so be sure to mount them securely. Use ⁵⁄₁₆-inch lag bolts and attach them to studs, not just drywall. You can also use these grids on the ceiling.

Lighter-weight grids

Grids made of thinner wire can hold small items over a workbench, or baskets filled with gloves and hats near the door to the house. You might need smaller screws to fit the brackets designed for these panels.

French cleat systems

With a table saw, you can make French cleats—a simple, low-cost option that lets you rearrange your storage almost as easily as if you used a manufactured system.

Cut a 45-degree bevel along a pair of strips, using 2 by 4s or void-free plywood at least ¾ by 3 inches. Make the strips as long as the cabinet's width. Screw one strip to wall studs with the beveled edge pointed up and out. Glue and screw the other piece to the cabinet's back, at the top, with the edge pointed down and out. The screws must penetrate the top and side edges of the cabinet, not just the flimsy back panel. Add a spacer as thick as the cleats to the bottom of the cabinet. You can then lift the cabinet into place. The cleat will  support it while you add a few screws where the cleat crosses studs to lock the unit into position. Use fasteners long enough to reach into the framing.

You can also cut long lengths of these strips and attach them like molding at levels where you might want to hang storage boxes or rows of hooks. Just attach a cleat to the accessory and then hang that cleat on one mounted to the wall. With lightweight items, you don't need to add screws to lock the second cleat into place.

LEFT: If you use a grid system as your basic organizing method, you can choose from a wide array of accessories, including shelves and shallow bins, as well as hooks for gear of all sizes.

RIGHT: Wire shelves are also available. This type, which is sturdy enough to hold heavy cans of paint, is supported by a built-in bracket that hooks into the grid at the back.

Pegboard

Before garage storage went upscale, there was pegboard. It fell out of favor in retail establishments because accessories don't grip the holes as securely as they do modern alternatives, such as slotwall or metal grids. But pegboard is enjoying a revival. It's inexpensive, easy to install, and widely available. And ¼-inch-thick pegboard is about as strong as MDF slotwall.

Embellishment

Before you install pegboard, you may want to paint it. Bright colors give it a fresh, stylish look. Julia Child, on a pegboard wall in her famous kitchen, painted the outlines of her pots so she'd know where to put them back. You can do the same with your tools.

Installation

Don't waste your time with ⅛-inch-thick pegboard. Buy the ¼-inch-thick type, which is much less likely to buckle or tear. First glue furring strips (thin pieces of molding about ½ by 1 inch) around the back perimeter. If the pegboard pieces are large, add a few vertical strips for reinforcement. Mark stud locations and then screw the panel on, going through the furring strips into studs. The molding creates a gap behind the board that is necessary for the hooks to grip.

If you use your garage workshop only occasionally, having key tools displayed before you on pegboard can be a great help.

Hidden pegboard

The wall behind a workbench isn't the only place to use pegboard. Here, it helps organize a closet full of garden tools. Be sure to install spacers behind the pegboard, just as you would if you were putting it on a wall.

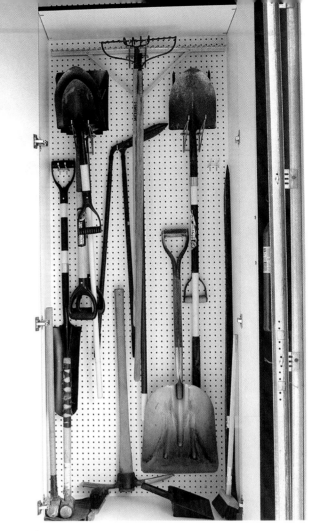

Hooks

Standard J-shaped hooks stay in place only because of a slight crook in the shaft. It's no wonder they often wobble or fall out. Stabilize them with snap-in peg locks *(left)*.

Longer hangers usually consist of a U-shaped piece spot-welded to an L-shaped bracket. If you need many hangers of this type, it's worth searching for a heavier-duty style with a back plate welded to the bracket in two places. This makes the hanger more stable.

Steel pegboard

For pegboard that can support heavy tools, look for panels made of steel. This kind is sold with snap-in holders and hangers.

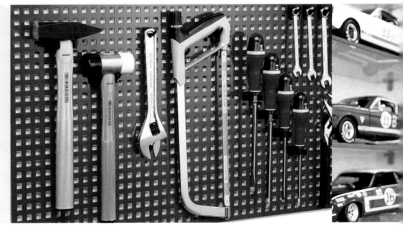

Wheels and casters

Some people add wheels to everything big that sits on the garage floor. It's one secret to getting a lot done in a small space. You wheel things out when you need them and zip them back when you're done. You can also clean more easily, and you don't have to worry that things might get wet from spills on the floor.

Adding casters

Many appliances and large tools are drilled for casters. In a garage, you'll probably want swivel casters on all four corners. This lets you instantly change direction and maneuver into tight spaces. For steering easily over long distances, put rigid casters on two corners and swivel casters on the others. The larger the wheels, the easier the item is to move and steer.

Locking casters

Most locking casters simply keep wheels from rolling. Total-lock casters also block the pivot. Install them on a table saw or other tool that you don't want moving on its own.

David Biondi wanted to squeeze a five-track model railroad into his two-car garage. Stringing track along the side and back walls was easy, but then he had to bridge the big garage door. His solution: He built a rolling platform for that section of track. When the railroad isn't running, he can move the platform and open the door.

No equipment sits on the floor in Cecil Ross's furniture-making studio; it all rolls. Without this feature, he figures, he'd need a shop twice as big.

Mobile bases

Consider installing a mobile base for heavy shop equipment. This is a set of locking casters attached to a frame that fits a machine's footprint. Some bases have a caster on each corner, while others have three casters—two on the back corners of the frame and one in the middle that drops down when you press on a foot pedal, allowing you to move the tool. Manufacturers list the specific tools that bases fit.

A mobile base allows woodworker David Beyl to scoot his heavy table saw and its auxiliary tables *(right)* around his garage when he needs to pull his car in or position the saw for cutting extra-long boards. The mobile base accommodates an auxiliary table on the side, but Beyl also needed an outfeed table behind the blade. So he rigged up a diagonal brace that goes along for the ride.

Storing big things

Finding space in a garage for cars, boats, and other large items presents certain challenges. Not only do the objects take up a lot of space, their shapes tend to block access to other things stored in a garage. You may find solutions by going up or out.

Car hoists

Car lifts let you store one vehicle on top of another. Wayne Haight keeps seven Ford muscle cars in a garage built to hold just six. A four-post lift provides the extra space, which he uses for a 1965 Cobra replica. Below the roadster, Haight parks a 1966 Mustang Fastback. On the right is a 1965 Sunbeam Tiger.

Parking aids

When you stow most things, you can immediately see whether they fit. But when you park a car, it isn't always so easy. Parking aids save you from driving too far into the garage or from stopping too short for the door to close. One type consists of a rubber-like mat that lets you feel a bump when it's time to stop. A higher-tech device aims a beam of red light on your dashboard when the vehicle is in the right spot. A homemade alternative: Dangle a tennis ball from a rope and stop when it hits your window.

Bumpers

If you maximize storage space along one wall, you may be left with a tight squeeze for a vehicle on the other side of the room. An inexpensive rubberlike bumper protects both the wall and your car doors.

Turntables

If your garage opens onto a busy street or a steep driveway, backing out can be scary. A turntable solves the problem. It automatically rotates your vehicle 360 degrees so that you can drive headfirst both ways. A turntable can be built into the floor as part of initial construction, but for about $5,000 (more for trucks and SUVs), you can add one to an existing garage. The system shown above includes a rotating table 12 feet in diameter, which takes up two car bays. You drive your car onto heavy steel pads that sit over track-mounted rollers, and a hydraulic gear drive spins the vehicle around. A different type of turntable, with an 8-foot diameter, is available for motorcycles.

Fold-down ledges

If you need to store large items only part of the time, you might want to mimic furniture maker John Thoe's fold-down ledges. The horizontal supports pivot on dowels threaded into the vertical supports, which are bolted to the wall. When Thoe needs shelf space, he raises a ledge and slips the diagonal braces into notches. When the shelf empties, he pulls out the braces and lowers the ledge. It stores flat against the wall.

Wall storage

Some people devote their entire garage to a pingpong table or fill a parking bay with a roof rack that's not in use. Linda and Dennis Nerstad store these oversized items flat against a wall. The pingpong table sits on two triangular shelf supports, and an elastic cord ties it to a hook at the top. The car-top carrier rides on hooks high up on the wall. When the Nerstads want to install the carrier on a vehicle, they just drive underneath and lower the unit into place.

Hanging storage

The Nerstads store lumber and a boat on chains and webbing that hang from hooks screwed into the support structure for the floor above. They set up this system under the eaves of their garage, but a similar setup would work indoors as well.

Pulley rigs

With a pulley system, you can store large items near the ceiling to preserve space below. Al Kitching and Katherine Kennedy built a rack *(left)* out of plywood and 2 by 4s that allows them to store two kayaks high on the back wall of their garage. The rigging consists of pulleys, rope, and a cleat, around which they wind the free end of the rope to keep the boats up.

You can also buy a pulley system *(below)* that works like mini-blinds. It has a built-in stop to keep items up. A gentle tug releases the mechanism so you can lower the object. Screw these pulleys directly to ceiling framing if the wood runs in the same direction you want to store things. Or attach the pulleys to plywood first and then screw the panels to the joists, as shown. You must use this method if the joists run crosswise to the pulley direction.

Floor stands

Children who ride bicycles often like to just drop them and run off. If you want to change this habit, consider getting a floor stand. Of all such storage devices, it's the easiest to use.

Support posts

You can also lean bicycles or other large gear against a post. If you add elastic cords or hooks, the bikes will be even more secure. For two-story storage on support posts, look in a bike shop. The post shown here holds up to four bicycles. It works best in garages with high ceilings.

Adjustable loft

Here's a solution for storing heavy over-sized items: a sturdy shelf that moves up and down with the push of a button. The shelf and hydraulic lift, similar to that in vehicle hoists, have a capacity of 1,000 pounds. Use this system to get snowmobiles, golf carts, lawn mowers, lumber, and other stuff out of the way. Expect to pay about $2,000.

Simple hooks

Inexpensive and effective, hooks screwed to a 2 by 4 *(right)* provide an amazing amount of storage space. Kevin Gnusti stores six bicycles in just 8 feet of wall space. Overhead, he hangs windsurfing equipment, a snowboard, and other lightweight gear in slings. The hooks extend into framing, not just drywall.

Shelves above doors

You can also store relatively lightweight oversized items on shelves that hang from the ceiling *(left)*. One prime spot for them is in the space above the track where the garage door rolls up. Wire shelving keeps the weight down and allows you to see what you've stored. The type shown comes with openings as wide as 8 feet—useful for long or bulky items. The shelves hang 18 to 45 inches down from the ceiling and hold up to 500 pounds each.

Chain hoist

The second story of Phil McCurdy's garage is devoted to storing car parts and doing specialty repair work, such as upholstery. Rather than carry heavy gear up the stairs, McCurdy rigged a half-ton chain hoist *(right)* to a steel beam that he installed near the roof as the garage was being built. He designed removable joists underneath the hoist for a section of the floor that separates the first and second stories. When McCurdy wants to use the hoist, he pulls up a cover on the floor, pops out the joist sections, and gets to work.

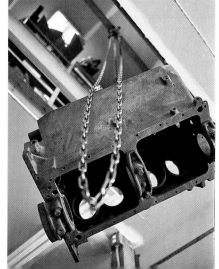

Storing little things

Whether craft materials or machine parts, little things tend to pile up in a garage. To quickly find what you need, you must store them in categories. The containers should be easy to use, encouraging you to put spare parts back where they belong every time.

Mini drawers and shelves

When you're storing baseball cards, stamps, nuts and bolts, or a wide array of other tiny parts, shallow drawers and shelves are especially handy because they help keep items from being piled up on one another. Woodworker David Beyl turned old cake pans into drawers for small hardware parts *(below, right)*. The drawers slide in shallow grooves that he cut on a tablesaw. Beyl made a similar unit, with thin shelves instead of pans, to organize sandpaper.

You can also purchase shallow trays made for storing tools *(below, left)*. They function just like Beyl's cake pans.

A third option *(above, right)* consists of metal drawer units with interchangeable inserts made of molded plastic. The inserts divide each drawer, creating four to 24 tiny compartments, depending on which insert you use.

Little boxes

You can also arrange small, open boxes across the bottom of a drawer. Buy plastic or wooden boxes or improvise with packaging you'd otherwise throw away. To recycle lightweight cardboard boxes as storage compartments, fold any flaps toward the interior to add strength.

Drawer dividers

When too many tools or parts rattle around in a drawer, dividers help bring order to the chaos. You can make your own from thin pieces of wood or plywood or buy them ready-made in wire, wood, or plastic. The dividers shown at right are made of beech. The dividers in the metal drawers below fit into slots on the bottom and along the sides of the drawer, allowing you to adjust the spacing in small increments.

Recycled containers

Food containers and many other types of packaging can also store small parts. The deli tray shown at right holds washers and other supplies.

Tin boxes

A model-railroad enthusiast recycles tins from flavored coffee drinks *(above)* to store supplies for miniature landscapes. The containers look tidy because they're identical. They use shelf space efficiently because they're rectangular, not round.

Stacking trays

Initially designed for builders to haul around in 5-gallon buckets, stacking trays now also come in sizes that fit 35-ounce coffee cans. In either size, these trays work great for storing small items that come in different sizes or styles, such as fasteners, fishing supplies, or craft materials. You can stack the trays on their own or in labeled buckets. For example, you might fill one bucket with trays containing screws and another with nails.

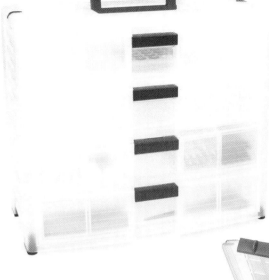

Portable organizers

Portable organizers are lidded boxes divided into small compartments. You can carry them into the house for a repair project or to a friend's house to work on a car. The organizer shown at right includes a lid with a grid pattern molded in. The grid keeps bin contents from spilling if the case tips.

Bins

In the business world, bins are the standard method for storing small parts. They're just as useful in a garage. Get plastic bins, which don't rust like metal or mildew like cardboard. Stack bins at the back of your workbench or set them in a row on a shelf. If you have too many to fit there, consider a bin cabinet or clip-on support rails. Store-fixture companies have a good selection.

Hardware cabinets

A hardware cabinet has rows of tiny drawers encased in a metal or plastic box. You can hang it on a wall or set it on a shelf. Look for drawers that are clear in front so you can see the contents. Some models have removable dividers within drawers, allowing you to subdivide categories.

Storing often used things

Things you use frequently should be visible and easy to reach. If something is easy to take out, it's also easy to put back.

Half-bowl holders

Jerry Kermode turns bowls and teaches wood turning in his garage, so he sometimes winds up with broken pieces. He cuts the good part of a broken bowl into a half-bowl and glues it to the wall, creating an elegant holder for scissors, calipers, and other small tools he uses often.

Tape-measure holder

Furniture maker John Thoe got tired of searching his shop for a tape measure, so he finally bought several. He screwed simple U-brackets to various workbenches and hangs the tape measures off them.

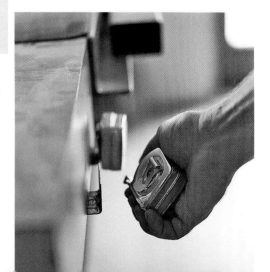

Open shelves

Even if you want most of your storage hidden behind doors or in drawers, open shelves often work best for things you use most. These shelves hold shoes that would otherwise collect on the floor next to a door that leads from the garage into the house. From the street, you see finished cabinets. But as you walk into the house, the shelves are right there and ready to use.

Mechanic's chair

Rolling chairs with built-in tool trays solve two problems at once. They hold your most used tools, and they prevent strain on your back and legs. This chair has two features not often found. It adjusts in height, and the raised lip provides lower-back support. A staple in auto-mobile repair shops, a mechanic's chair comes in handy whenever you need to keep tools at hand as you move around within your garage.

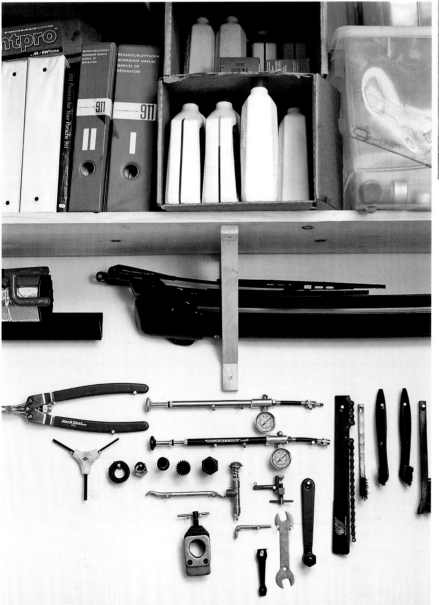

Clip and hang

Some commonly used tools have design features that invite clever storage solutions. For example, try storing spring clamps by clipping them to one another and hanging them in strings.

Nail system

With a few nails, Kevin Gnusti created a storage wall for his most used bicycle tools. It functions like pegboard, slot-wall, or gridwall, but the cost was minuscule. Above his workbench tool display, he stores repair manuals and gear. The shelf rests on a wooden sup-port. Its triangular opening doubles as a holder for windshield wipers, fishing poles, and other long, thin items.

Specialty hangers

Whatever you need to store, chances are there is a specialty hanger that can help you do it. You can attach some types directly to the wall, using either screws or fasteners made to grip drywall or hallow concrete blocks. Other types clip into pegboard, grid systems, or slotwall. If you find a hanger with an attachment system you can't use, ask whether adapter hardware exists.

RIGHT: Hangers for golf gear typically contain hooks or baskets for shoes as well as a place to hang bags.

BELOW: Ladder hooks are wide and long, so you can also use them to store wheelbarrows, extension cords, lightweight outdoor furniture, and other bulky items you want to keep off the floor.

ABOVE: One of many approaches to storing garden tools, this system features soft-tipped prongs that grip onto shovels, rakes, and other long-handled equipment.

LEFT: By allowing you to store bicycles vertically against a wall, this hook saves space. The hook's design also helps protect the wall from scuffs.

RIGHT: This rack holds sports rackets of any type. Depending on the kind, it stores up to seven, plus two cans of tennis balls.

LEFT: With this hook, you need just a few inches of wall space to store a pair of skis and poles. You could even hang your goggles here.

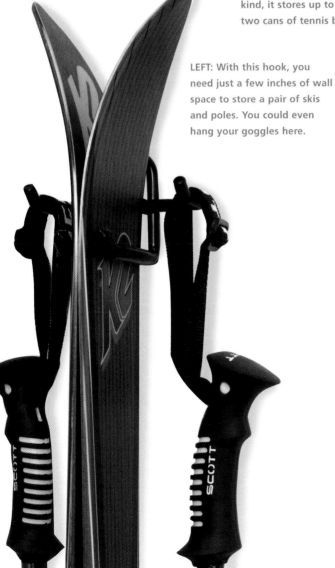

ABOVE: With a variety of slots and hooks, this organizer stores the hand tools you're likely to use most often.

Storing seldom used things

When you reserve prime storage space for your most used items, the stuff you use only occasionally often needs to go where it's harder to reach. Focus on making access to these areas as easy as possible.

Library ladder

When a house is built with high ceilings, the garage often winds up with them as well. Floor-to-ceiling cabinets make good use of this space. A library ladder saves you from having to haul out a standard one each time you need it. This ladder rides on a rail that bends to get around a column midpoint on the wall.

Two-story storage

Furniture maker Cecil Ross works with unusual wood. He sometimes stores slabs for several years while they dry. When the wood is ready, he wants it to be buried under as few other pieces as possible. By dividing his storage area in half vertically, he keeps his stacks short.

Shelves between trusses

The roof of this garage *(left)* is framed with trusses, which split the attic into small sections. The homeowner closed in the ceiling in strips, creating a series of shelves. Rather than store items in categories, he numbers each section and keeps an inventory of the contents. Bin 5 holds fishing reels, hard hats, skis, an easel, crutches, and Venetian blinds—a collection he'd never remember without his list.

Storage loft

Joe Driscoll's garage has a high, open ceiling unencumbered by truss framing, so he took advantage of the space by building a loft to store seldom used items. Now everything is off the floor so he has room for a model train set (under the plastic tarp to keep dust off). His pulley system is for bicycles that are rarely used. To get them down, he has to maneuver them around the storage cabinet underneath.

OUTFITTING

CHAPTER

TWO

YOUR GARAGE

Once you've organized your things, you may want to upgrade certain systems in your garage to make it suitable for other activities. In some cases, a good workbench and improved lighting may suffice. Others may need heating and ventilation, or new doors. As you'll see in this chapter, no garage needs to remain a dark, drafty space when it can be filled with light, warmth, and energy.

Workbenches

No matter how you use your garage, you'll most likely need at least one work surface. It might be a small countertop for doing minor household repairs or bicycle tune-ups. Or it could be a big, heavy woodworking bench. Whatever the function, key issues include height, heft, and relationship to the rest of your garage.

PORTABLE WORKBENCH

might want several work surfaces. Federal guidelines for laboratory workers are good for garage workbenches too:

- For precision work, make the bench above elbow height.
- For light work, set it just below elbow height.
- For heavy work, aim for 4 to 6 inches below elbow height.

Heft

A lightweight work surface is fine for rewiring a lamp or assembling toys. But if you're nailing something together, a heavy, stable workbench makes you much more efficient. Try nailing directly over a leg, where even a flimsy work surface is most rigid, and you'll see what a difference it makes.

LEFT: Made from 2 by 4s and 2 by 6s bolted together, this simple bench provides the essentials for supporting general household repairs: a sturdy surface, convenient tool storage, and a machinist's vise. The vise, bolted to the bench end with the most clearance, provides an extra hand when needed.

Height

If you buy a workbench, it's likely to be 33 to 36 inches high. But that's not necessarily right for you. The best height allows you to stand as straight as possible while you work on projects and still get the leverage you need for the task at hand. If your activities vary—especially if you spend a lot of time working in your garage—you

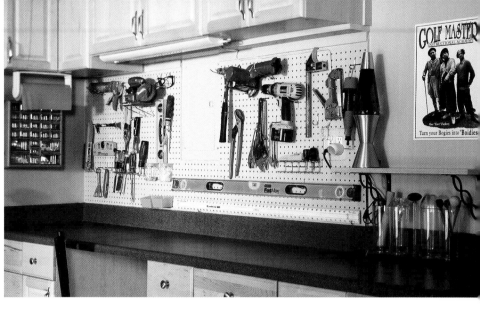

Placement

Kitchen designers plan countertop space around a work triangle that links the stove, sink, and refrigerator. A similar approach can help you best situate your workbench.

- Place it near the cabinets, walls, or shelves where you store your tools.
- Put it under good light.
- Avoid placing it near a door to the house, where it will be more likely to collect clutter.

Countertop workbench

If you use your workbench mostly for light household repairs, consider a standard kitchen-style countertop *(above)*. Choose laminate, metal, butcher block, or even ordinary plywood or particleboard.

Portable workbench

A fold-down, portable workbench may be all you need. The model shown *(opposite page, top)* is similar to the first portable workbench, introduced in the 1960s. This new version supports up to 550 pounds and has a three-part top: a removable center panel and two sidepieces that operate as a vise.

Metal workbench

A metal workbench, such as the one shown below, may include drawers and shelves and even a wooden countertop.

Woodworker's bench

If you do a lot of woodworking and have space in your garage, you'll appreciate having a traditional bench. You can buy complete benches, such as the $1,000 model shown at left, or build one yourself, either from scratch or from components that are partially or fully assembled. Don't waste money on a cheap bench of this type; it's better to make do with a temporary solution and portable bench until you can afford something solid enough to hold wood steady while you work.

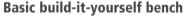

WOODWORKER'S BENCH

Basic build-it-yourself bench

This easy-to-build workbench *(right)* with a pegboard back consists mostly of 2 by 4s connected with metal brackets similar to those used in wood house framing. There are no fancy joints or angles to cut and no holes to bore. Self-drilling screws hold everything together.

METAL WORKBENCH

BASIC
BUILD-IT-YOURSELF
BENCH

Carver's bench

For carving and other detail work, a bench like furniture maker John Thoe's is hard to beat. The top is about elbow height. He can rest one forearm on the bench to control a cut and lean into the other arm with his whole body to push the blade into the wood. A window floods the workbench with light.

Chest-high bench

When jeweler Jane Martin makes intricate cuts, she works nearly at face level, using a shelf above an old wooden desk as her workbench. She clamps a V-shaped brace to the shelf to support thin metal pieces and keep them from bending while she cuts with a fine-tooth jeweler's saw.

Sawhorses and doors

For workbenches that need to be big but not necessarily strong, a simple and affordable solution is shown below. Carol Olsen, a fabric artist, uses lightweight workbenches that she painted in cheery colors. For legs, she attached 2 by 4s to sawhorse hardware. For tops, she bought inexpensive hallow-core doors, which are lightweight and remarkably sag resistant. She covered one door with a pad to create a spacious ironing board.

Foldout bench

If your garage doesn't have room for a full-scale workbench, consider units that fold out from a wall. The bench shown at right provides relatively generous work space, 28 by 43$\frac{1}{2}$ inches, and comes with both shoulder and tail vises. Yet it sticks out a mere 10 inches when folded down. For stability, this bench should be bolted to the wall.

Murphy bed hinges

Using the fold-down hardware of a Murphy bed, the designer of the custom cabinets at left created a super-sturdy workbench in a garage that's just deep enough for a car to park. Murphy beds typically depend on their two front legs to keep the mechanism from dumping everything onto the floor. But this bench gets by without any legs. A horizontal pipe above the mechanism acts as a stop.

Giant drawing tablet

Many garage projects start with sketches and measurements. Furniture maker Cecil Ross goes a step further. Using boatbuilders' methods, he creates full-scale drawings and then cuts parts to match. Because he topped his bench with a full sheet of melamine-coated particleboard, Ross can sketch an idea and wipe it away if it doesn't work. He designed the curved armrest of the chair shown above by using a flexible rule and a set of "whales," weights used by boat builders.

Mini kitchen

Base cabinets equipped with a deep sink and a dishwasher can help turn a garage into a multipurpose room suitable for entertaining as well as flower arranging. In this garage *(right)*, the cabinets and refrigerator line one sidewall so there's still room to park cars.

Built-in grid

Workbenches can double as measurement tools. When Carolyn Brown set up her garage as an upholstery shop, she covered one large worktable with plastic mats designed for use with rotary cutters. Brown also uses the mats when she cuts with scissors. The yellow grid lines help keep her cuts square and accurate.

Glider bench

Auxiliary workbenches sometimes have rollers to help support and move long, heavy pieces. But standard cylindrical rollers move in only two directions. They aren't as versatile or easy to use as roller balls, which rotate freely on ball bearings.

Shelf support

You can also create an adjustable work surface with shelf standards and brackets, as David Beyl did on the base of his drill press. When he wants a table, he hooks on brackets and supports a shelf on them. To adjust the height, he moves the brackets. If you need a temporary work surface at one set height, try fold–down shelf brackets as supports instead.

Adjustable legs

With adjustable legs, a workbench can always be at an ideal height. The legs of the bench shown at left consist of nesting steel frames that slide out $16\frac{1}{2}$ inches, with 12 stops along the way. A ratcheting mechanism controls the stops. Another option is an adjustable workstation or workbench found in a store that specializes in used office and industrial equipment.

Lighting

Garage lighting has come a long way. Nowadays, no one needs to settle for flickering, greenish fluorescent tubes that take forever to light when the weather is cold. Better options include flicker-free fluorescents, task lights of many types, and new ways of bringing in natural light.

Incandescent bulbs

If you use your garage only to park a car and store recyclables, a single incandescent bulb may be best. It goes on instantly and burns at full power no matter the temperature. Cheap fluorescent shop lights, on the other hand, may flicker or not even start if the weather is cold. Bulbs switched on for only a few minutes each day don't use much energy, regardless of their type.

Fluorescent tubes

If you plan to use your garage for extended periods, great fluorescents will give you the best overall lighting. Choose fixtures that take T8 tubes and have electronic ballasts. They cost more than basic shop lights, which hold T12 bulbs and magnetic ballasts, but they're worth it for several reasons. (T means "tubular," and the number refers to diameter in eighths of an inch. So T8s are 1 inch wide, while T12s are 1½ inches wide.)

A shop light over David Biondi's workbench provides bright light for the detail work involved in his hobby of building model railroads. Placing the fixture close to the workbench and slightly to the front, so his body doesn't cast a shadow on his work, lets him take advantage of the full intensity of the light.

- T8s with electronic ballasts produce about the same light as T12s but use 32 percent less energy.
- T8 tubes render colors more accurately and don't fade as noticeably as they age.
- Electronic ballasts prevent flickering, don't hum, and work at lower temperatures, usually down to zero degrees Fahrenheit. Energy-saver T12 tubes with magnetic ballasts don't operate correctly below 60 degrees, a real problem in many garages.
- Rapid-start ballasts, the most common kind, generally work better in garages than instant-start ballasts. When lights are switched on and off frequently, as they are in most garages, instant-start ballasts burn out tubes prematurely.
- Fixtures that take 4-foot tubes are better than ones for 8-foot tubes. The shorter tubes are less expensive, easier to handle, longer lasting, and more energy efficient.
- For basic lighting, aim to create even illumination across your garage. One fixture every 4 feet is better than two every 8 feet.

Often the best garage lighting comes from a variety of sources. Here, natural light from windows is supplemented with fluorescent fixtures filled with tubes that produce several colors to get the most even color day and night. Incandescent fixtures are used as task lights for detail work.

Seeing colors accurately

Once you decide on a fixture, you can then select a bulb or tube that produces the best light for your needs. Consider two factors: whether the light looks cool or warm (which affects ambiance) and whether it makes objects appear their true color (which affects your ability to match a patch to surrounding wood or to appreciate the color of your blue Porsche).

- The ambiance factor is determined by a bulb or tube's color temperature, expressed as degrees on the Kelvin scale. Neutral light (3500K) usually works well in most garages. However, if you use your garage as a music studio or entertainment area, you might want warm light (3000K). For an office look, cool light (4100K) would be better. Some people find that cooler light lets them see fine details more crisply. Color temperature is listed on packages.
- Color rendering, a bigger issue in many garages, is expressed as a bulb or tube's color rendition index, or CRI. The higher the score, the truer the colors. A CRI score of 100, so far possible only with halogen incandescents, means colors theoretically appear as they do in sunlight. T12s score in the 60s, while T8s and T5s often rate about 85. Most people think colors look great at 85 and above. Below 80, they often look odd.

Task lights

Task lights focus bright light where you need it most. When you install them, think about where shadows will fall and whether the light will shine into your eyes.

Desk lights

Clip-on desk lights make ideal task lights in a garage. Wood turner Jerry Kermode *(right)* rigged one next to his lathe so that the light focuses on his work without getting in his eyes.

Under-cabinet fixtures

Under-cabinet lights work as well for task lighting in a garage as they do in a kitchen, but the issues are a bit different. There are two categories: fluorescents and incandescents, which include halogen and xenon bulbs.

Fluorescents: Fluorescents use T4 or T5 tubes, so the fixtures are extremely thin, often only about an inch high and wide. In kitchens, their big dis-

advantage is that they can't be dimmed. In a garage, that's usually not an issue. Fluorescents produce less heat than other options, and they are the most energy efficient. For good light all along a workbench with shelves or cabinets above, fluorescents are an

excellent choice. Many types of under-cabinet lights clip together to make a continuous strip.

Incandescents: Incandescents' more focused beam may reduce eyestrain if you do highly detailed work.

■ Halogens, which are incandescents of a special type, produce the brightest, most focused light, but they also generate considerable heat. For use under cabinets, buy only low-voltage fixtures, which have built-in transformers that keep heat down. The focused beam may allow you to use less light than you would need with other types of under-counter lights. So the overall effect in your garage could be a lower electrical bill and more pleasant work conditions.

■ Xenon bulbs are incandescents with a little xenon gas added to lengthen the life of the bulb. They are a good choice if you want incandescents without the heat of halogens.

Display lights

About 100 miniature bulbs illuminate the model railroad track that winds on two levels around the garage shown above. To keep the lights from shining in people's eyes, the bulbs and wiring are tucked under a shelf with a lip.

Magnifier lights

A magnifying lens with a built-in light is great for detail work.

Track lights

When this one-car garage was converted into an art studio, the homeowner added a skylight and track lights. Along with the white walls and wood floor, they give the space the clean, bright look of an art gallery.

Skylights

Nothing beats natural light. But garage walls tend to have few or no windows. Clever solutions, however, help you get around this fact. The owner of the garage below added skylights to the roof and hung fluorescent fixtures between them. During the day, the skylights give plenty of light; at night, the fluorescents fill in.

Light tubes: A light tube is a skylight that causes light waves to bounce back and forth as they descend through a tube with reflective walls. This funnels bright light into interior space even where the roof is slanted away from direct sun. Because the tube flexes, it directs light to a specific spot, almost as if it were a light fixture. If your garage has a finished ceiling, light tubes are far simpler to install than traditional skylights because you don't need to build a shaft to direct light down. Some tubes have bulbs that you can switch on when it's dark outside.

Greenhouse bump-out

Tom Spivey brought light into his one-car garage and added a small greenhouse at the same time. He cut a hole in a sidewall and framed a series of triangular braces to support a ledge where he keeps frost-sensitive plants over the winter. Windows salvaged from a remodeling project bring in light.

Smart space planning

To take best advantage of natural light, do detail work near a window or door whenever possible. In Cecil Ross' garage *(below),* tools are sharpened next to two big windows. The bright light helps him detect when an edge is sharp, because at that point, the fine line of metal separating front and back surfaces disappears.

David Beyl *(right)* set up his lathe near his garage door. Wood turners typically do all their sanding while a piece is still on the lathe. Only with excellent light can they tell whether any scratches or nicks remain.

Heating

Depending on where you live, adding heat to your garage can be either a luxury or an essential feature that allows you to use the space year-round. As with any heating project, the first steps should be to add insulation and plug air leaks. Then you can install a heater that will work best for you.

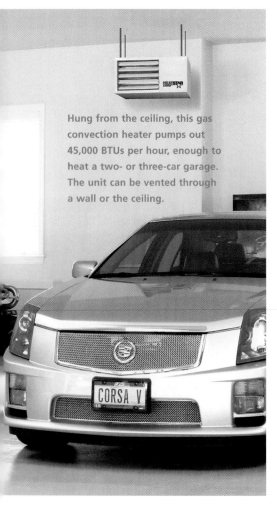

Hung from the ceiling, this gas convection heater pumps out 45,000 BTUs per hour, enough to heat a two- or three-car garage. The unit can be vented through a wall or the ceiling.

There are two basic types of heaters: convection heaters, which blow hot air, and radiant heaters, which use infrared heat waves to warm objects directly. Both types come in electric and gas versions. A wood-burning stove may also make sense, especially if you do a lot of woodworking and generate scraps. If you're designing a garage from scratch, in-floor radiant heat is also an option.

Gas vs. electric: Natural gas units are generally less expensive to run than electric heaters but are more costly to install. With gas heaters, you have a choice between ventless and vented models. Ventless units are easier to install and more energy efficient, but you breathe the combustion by-products, which may include carbon monoxide. And with a ventless unit, water vapor released by burning natural gas or propane also stays inside, which can cause your tools to rust. The more airtight your garage, the more you should opt for a vented heater, which exhausts combustion gases and water vapor outdoors, usually through a wall. Electric heaters don't produce exhaust or release water vapor, so they don't need to be vented.

Convection heaters

Convection heaters made for garages blow warm air, just as forced-air systems do in a house, but without ducts. If you do a lot of dusty activities, such as woodworking, a convection heater might not be the best choice because it will blow the dust around. However, if you have forced-air heating in your house, this may be the type of heating you prefer. Electric heaters big enough to heat a garage usually require a 220-volt circuit.

Radiant heaters

With a radiant heater (*opposite page, top left*), you feel warmth almost immediately. There is no fan to make noise or blow dust around. Small electric models, which plug into standard outlets, often heat only about 200 square feet—a workbench area, not an entire garage. Large models require 220-volt circuits. Gas heaters are generally less expensive to operate, so it's no surprise that they are the most popular option. Most of these aren't vented, so installation usually involves

This electric convection heater is available in various sizes, capable of heating one- to three-car garages. Like other convection heaters, it relies on its built-in fan to circulate warm air throughout the garage.

just extending a gas line and screwing on support brackets.

Vented, gas-powered radiant heaters cost more but keep combustion gases and moisture out of your garage. In the model below, a double-walled tube extends through a wall. Air needed for combustion flows in through a small pipe in the center, and hot exhaust air exits through the bigger pipe on the outside. Because all the operational parts are completely enclosed, a vented radiant heater is a particularly good choice if there is a lot of dust in your garage.

Effective placement: Working directly under a radiant heater can seem pleasant at first. But if you do it for too long, your brain can feel baked. Aim small heaters at your workbench and direct larger heaters to warm the floor behind you. The floor will then radiate heat up to you.

VENTED GAS RADIANT HEATER

Portable heaters

A two-car garage can require 25,000 BTUs to heat in some climates, far beyond the capacity of most portable heaters. But if your weather is relatively mild and your garage is well insulated, a portable electric heater or two may be all you need. The safest options keep the surface temperature low enough so a fire can't start if a heater tips over. Good choices include ceramic heaters, which use a fan to draw air through a heated element, oil-filled radiator-style heaters, and Micathermic heaters, which have an electrical coil in the middle that heats sheets of mica.

This Micathermic portable heater switches on and off in response to a remote-control thermostat that the owner keeps on the desk in her garage office. Locating the thermostat there ensures a comfortable working environment where she spends the most time.

In-floor heat

In-floor radiant heat, which channels warm water through pipes within a concrete slab, is the ultimate way to warm a garage. You get silent, steady, uniform heat with no blowing air and no impact on the air quality in your garage. But there are caveats:

■ In-floor radiant heat must be installed when the floor is poured. Electric mats that go under tile bring this kind of heating to remodeled bathrooms, but they aren't powerful enough to heat a garage.

■ In-floor radiant heat is very efficient, but only when you compare it with other methods used over the same period. Radiant heat isn't something you switch on and off for short periods. It takes a long time to heat a cold slab of concrete. If you're in your garage only occasionally, a system that heats up quickly would be more economical.

When Philip McCurdy retired from the Navy, he decided to start a new career doing something he loves: restoring antique cars. Now he spends nearly every day in his garage, which he built with in-floor radiant heat. He considers the heating system one of the best features of his building, which is loaded with details that would make most garage lovers envious. He set the thermostat to 63 degrees—his perfect working temperature—and left it there.

Dealing with household systems

Many garages contain the house's furnace, water heater, and other equipment. If you're spiffing up your garage, you can create a closet to keep such units out of sight. If any of the equipment operates on gas, however, be careful not to cut off an air supply. Use louvered doors or pipe in fresh air. A heating company should check to ensure that the air supply is adequate.

ABOVE: This garage's machine room keeps equipment out of sight yet easy to get to for repairs and maintenance.

BELOW: This cabinet hides a whole-house vacuum. A long hose, which allows the machine to double as a shop vac, goes in the drawer below.

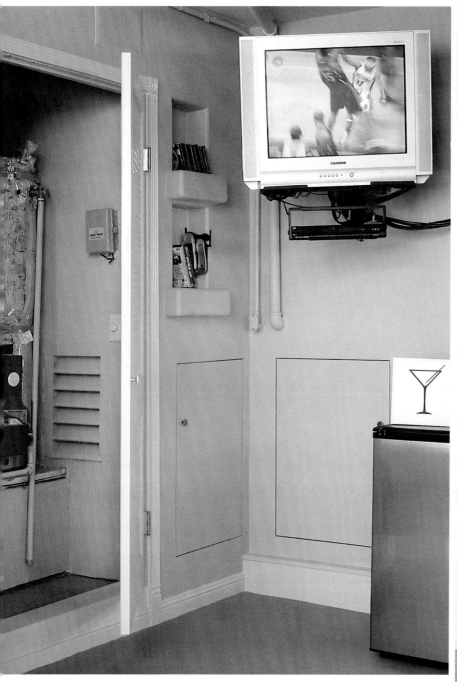

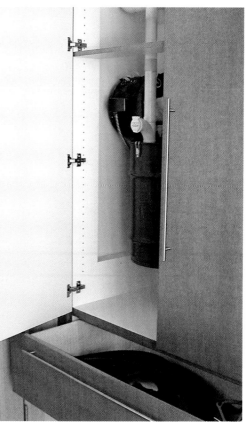

ABOVE: When one homeowner enclosed his house's gas furnace, he added a vent to draw combustion air from the crawl space behind the wall to the right. The small doors to the right of the furnace give him access to the crawl space.

Ventilation

Some garage owners never need to worry about ventilation. Their garages leak so much air that ventilation happens on its own. But bringing in fresh air and venting dirty air become bigger concerns as you close off air leaks, add heat, and spend more time in your garage.

Screen doors

Opening the garage door is an obvious way to bring in fresh air. But if you're concerned about bugs, debris, or neighborhood pets, consider adding a screen door. Some garage screen doors slide on tracks and stack on either side *(below)*. You can still drive into both bays of a two-car garage, but you have to move the doors in between. Other sliding doors pull down *(right),* like window shades, from a cassette mounted at the top of the door opening. Roll-up screens are a third option. The screen hangs from hook-and-loop material and includes zippered openings so you can walk in and out while the screen is down. When you don't need the screen, just roll it up.

Exhaust fans

For getting rid of nasty fumes, a combination of strategies usually works best because exhaust fans aren't as efficient as fans that blow air. Jeweler Jane Martin uses a crock-pot with a tight-fitting lid *(above)* to confine gases that form when she soaks metal pieces in acids to create patina finishes. She traps whatever gases escape by using one of her homemade fume collectors. One system consists of an in-line fan, a dryer vent pipe, and an old light fixture. Another is an old kitchen range hood taped to a cardboard box *(right),* with flaps that act as doors. The makeshift setup functions like expensive vented enclosures in laboratories.

Operable windows

Many garages have windows that don't open, as if all fresh air is meant to come in through the big garage door. But when a garage opens onto a busy street, an operable sidewall window provides ventilation without compromising noise control or privacy. This window was retrofitted so it pivots open on casement adjusters.

Dust control

Many garage activities generate dust or fumes that you don't want to inhale. For a safer, cleaner shop, you need to corral them. Strategies vary from wearing the right kind of mask to using dust-collection systems and exhaust fans.

Masks

They're not the best long-term solution, but disposable masks do keep sawdust out of your lungs. Avoid single-band kinds labeled "dust mask." They don't seal well and won't protect you. Look for two elastic bands and the word "respirator" on the package.

■ To filter out sawdust, you need an N95 respirator, meaning it takes out at least 95 percent of nonoily particles (dust, mists, and fumes). For lead dust and other especially hazardous particles, get an N99, which takes out 99 percent of particles, or an N100, which stops 99.97 percent.

■ For oily particles or droplets, such as lubricants or spray-on oil finishes, buy a respirator with a code starting with R (resistant to oil) or P (oil-proof).

■ Some disposable respirators incorporate charcoal filters to block minor amounts of fast-evaporating solvents and other gases. If the concentration is more than a nuisance level, however, you need a rubberized half- or full-face mask with cartridges rated for the chemicals you are using. Most solvents require organic-vapor cartridges. But check labels on products. If they require good ventilation but don't advise using a respirator, it's probably because a respirator won't block that chemical formula.

Fresh-air hoods

Standard respirators don't work if you wear a beard or have a health condition that requires you to breathe with unrestricted airflow. And masks aren't efficient if you turn wood or tackle other jobs that generate lots of dust. In these situations, you need a powered respirator—a hood and face shield filled with air that's been pulled through a filter by a battery-powered blower. The positive pressure keeps out dust. Prices start at less than $300.

Some powered respirators tuck the mechanics into a visor. Others, like the one shown above, enclose the fan, filter, and rechargeable battery in a small box that you wear on your belt.

Wood turner Jerry Kermode buys Tyvek hoods and face shields that go with a commercial unit. The rest of his system is homemade. He connects the hood to a flexible pipe and a fan that gently blows in fresh air. In summer, he taps air outside his garage, and in winter, he pipes in warm air from his house.

Cyclone collectors

If you use a shop vac as a dust collector with a planer or other messy tool, you'll discover that the canister fills very quickly. Installing a cyclone collector *(right)* between the vacuum and your tool will allow you to work longer at a stretch. This collector consists of a special lid over a standard garbage can. The lid's shape sends sawdust swirling in a circular path, causing big pieces to drop out into the can. Only very fine particles wind up in the vacuum.

Dedicated dust-collection systems

The ultimate solution is a plumbed-in dust-collection system in which lengths of pipe connect tools to a central vacuum. There's an art to designing this type of system, so take a list of your tools and the dimensions of your garage with you when you shop. Make ducts as short and as straight as possible so you don't sap the vacuum's power. Instead of 90-degree turns, make gentle curves with pairs of 45-degree connectors. If you use plastic pipe, install a ground wire to control static electricity.

In this garage, piping for a dust collector is built into the walls. The dust collector itself is housed in a cabinet outside so the owner doesn't have to listen to the motor or breathe dust that seeps through the collection bag.

Shop vacs

If you use your garage for woodworking or other dusty activities, using a shop vac or a dust-collection device is the simplest way to keep the air clean. An increasing number of tools have built-in ports for easy hookup. If your tools lack this feature, build a collection chute or work on a plywood base drilled with holes and vacuum dust downward.

Use a shop vac rated to HEPA (High Efficiency Particle Arrestor) standards, which means it filters 99.97 percent of the fine dust that can damage your lungs. Replacement filters *(above)* that fit most shop vacs allow you to upgrade without buying a new machine. Look for a filter that you can rinse off and reuse.

Air filters

Several companies market air filters designed to clean air in a garage. These devices use a fan and furnace-style filters to collect dust. While the filter may keep your garage cleaner, it collects dust that's already in the air—the same air you're breathing. Don't count on an air filter as your main defense.

Housekeeping strategies

Your garage may not need a full-blown dust-collection or exhaust system, but there are still steps you can take to help keep the space as tidy as possible.

Dust cover

Joe Driscoll uses his garage for model railroads, which run on a rollout display stored along one wall. Between sessions, Driscoll focuses on keeping the tiny parts free of dust. He covers everything with plastic, which rolls out on a support system he built with shelf brackets and thin pieces of wood. Inside the plastic, Driscoll runs a small air filter.

Easy cleanup

Think about sweeping or vacuuming when you set up your garage. Instead of supporting work surfaces on four legs, you can attach them to triangular braces bolted to wall studs. The braces leave the floor free of obstructions, so it's easy to clean.

Separate rooms

If you have room, you might want to divide your garage so you can confine messes to one area. Cecil Ross built a wall to create a small gallery space at one end of his garage, where he builds furniture *(right)*.

Keith Bowen, who restores bassoons, created two shower-sized enclosures at one end of his garage *(below, left)*. In one stall, he buffs metal parts. He applies finishes in the other space, which is equipped with an exhaust fan to the outdoors.

Philip McCurdy, who restores antique cars, installed a barn-style sliding door, which functions as a movable wall that allows him to divide his garage in half *(below, right)*.

Safety

However a garage functions, it's probably also the catchall for products that are too smelly or flammable to be stored safely in living areas: paint strippers, stains, thinners, insecticides, fertilizers, pool and spa chemicals, cleaners, gasoline for a lawn mower. It might also house a car that drips oil. Safety is an obvious concern.

House-to-garage connection

To keep a garage fire from roaring into an attached house, building codes require that the garage side of the wall be covered with fire-resistant drywall. There cannot be any openings or vents that might funnel fire into the house. The connecting door must be fire rated, which usually means solid wood 1 3/8 inches thick. The hardware must allow the door to close on its own. If you compromise any of these features, perhaps by adding a pet door, move flammables out and treat the garage more like living space. Plan to reverse your changes if you ever put the house up for sale.

Vapor control

Many flammable liquids give off vapors that are heavier than air. To keep them from drifting into the house, the connecting doorway must step up at least 4 inches from the garage floor. Building codes also require water heaters and furnaces to sit on platforms at least 18 inches high so that the pilot lights and electrical elements are safely above any flammable vapors. Maintain these heights if you remodel. When vapors are heavier than air, you can't count on your sense of smell to warn you when something has gone wrong.

Fire extinguishers

A fire extinguisher allows you to put out a small fire, but only if it's the right type in the right place and if you know how to use it properly. Some extinguishers sold for kitchen and garage use handle only fires of Class B (flammable liquids) and Class C

A cabinet built to hide household equipment incorporates important safety features. A built-in platform keeps the water heater and furnace safely above any flammable vapors. Louvered doors provide the fresh air needed for gas combustion. And the doors open wide for easy maintenance.

(energized electrical equipment). Opt instead for an ABC type, which also stops fires in ordinary combustibles, such as paper, wood, and plastic. Numbers in the rating refer to the quantity of material and therefore the size of fire you may be able to stop; 2A10BC is a good size for a garage. Mount the extinguisher within sight and easy reach near an outside door. It could be a long time before you use the extinguisher, so post this reminder on how to use it:

- ■ **P**ull the pin to unlock the handle.
- ■ **A**im low into the fire.
- ■ **S**queeze the handle.
- ■ **S**weep from side to side.

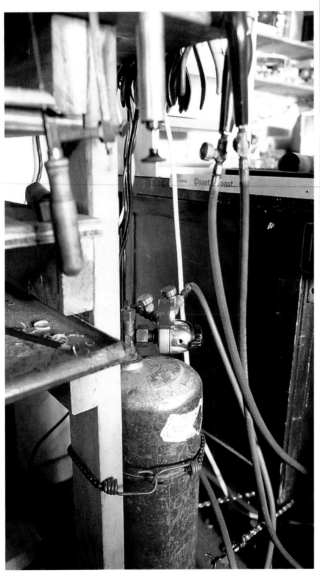

Fire-safe workbench

Joining metal pieces often involves high temperatures, whether you're soldering, welding, or braising. Working on a fireproof workbench is essential. Keith Bowen, who restores about 500 bassoons a year in his garage, works on recycled firebricks when he braises keys and other parts *(above)*. The bricks rest on a flattened metal duct to catch any drips of molten solder. Above the bench is a window, which Bowen opens for ventilation when his torch is lit.

Tip-over protection

Jeweler Jane Martin also uses silver-soldering techniques, but with an acetylene torch. So that she or an earthquake won't tip the tank, she secured it to the leg of a workbench with an elastic cord *(left)*.

Oily rags

Linseed oil, found in many finishes, cures into a plasticlike finish by combining with oxygen in the air. The chemical change gives off enough heat to ignite oily rags if they are left wadded up in the garage. Place oily or solvent-laden rags in a metal container with a tight-fitting lid, like the ones shown below, until you can hang them on a line outside. If the rags are oily but not soaked with solvent, you can also launder them or dampen them with water, wrap them in plastic, and toss them into the trash.

Carbon monoxide

Most people know that warming up a car in a closed garage will fill the air with carbon monoxide. But even with the garage door open, this gas can seep through the connecting wall into the house, particularly if there is a dryer or exhaust fan operating indoors. Installing a small exhaust fan in the garage guards against this possibility. Wire the fan to the garage door opener so that the fan runs about 10 minutes each time the door opens or closes.

Carbon monoxide detectors:
A carbon monoxide detector inside the house can alert you to even small concentrations of this gas. But manufacturers warn not to use one in a garage. The detector might sound an alarm too often, and its sensor might be damaged by other gases given off by car engines. The best option is simply never to run combustion devices inside the garage. If you must work on gasoline engines in your garage, consider investing in the same type of warning device that parking garages and machine shops use, a carbon monoxide monitor and ventilation fan controller. This type of monitor is expensive, but if it detects an unacceptable carbon monoxide level, it sounds an alarm and activates an exhaust fan.

Heat detectors

Particularly if your garage is attached to your house, you should install an electronic monitor to warn people to flee if a fire starts in the garage. But smoke detectors like those you'd use inside your house aren't usually the best choice for the garage, because dust from woodworking or similar activities can trigger false alarms. Two other types of monitors—heat detectors and flame detectors—don't have this problem. Flame detectors cost more, so heat detectors are the best choice in most garages.

Pesticides and other hazardous materials

If you store pesticides and other hazardous materials in your garage, you must devise a storage method that makes them inaccessible to children. In addition, you need an area that is dry, well ventilated, and protected against temperature extremes. Providing all of this at once is difficult, especially if the garage is attached

Vented storage

Even with a safety cabinet, you'll smell vapors each time you open the door. To get around this, vent the cabinet outside. Consult the fire department for local regulations. Industry-approved setups generally involve a metal duct leading outdoors from a bottom vent, as chemical vapors tend to be heavier than air. Replacement air comes through a top vent.

Outdoor storage

When garages were simple backyard sheds, they served well for keeping smelly, flammable products. But such materials don't belong in a modern garage used almost as part of the house. A stand-alone, lockable storage unit *(below)* outdoors may be preferable, at least where freezing isn't likely.

to the house. To avoid temperature extremes, you might need to heat or air-condition the garage even as you leave a vent open or a fan running for ventilation. There are better options.

Store as little as possible: One survey found that 25 percent of pesticides purchased for home use wind up sitting unused in the garage or under the kitchen sink. Before you buy a pesticide, solvent, or other hazardous material, read the label and make sure you need the product and feel comfortable using it. Many low-toxic alternatives exist these days. If you must use a product labeled as a health or fire risk, ask friends or neighbors whether you can use their leftovers. If you do buy, get only as much as you expect to use within a year. Some formulas break down over time or change if temperatures dip below 40 degrees or rise above 85 degrees.

Safety cabinets

Lockable metal cabinets *(above)* are the best place to store pesticides and flammable materials. Top-of-the-line industrial models are not cheap, but they have many safety features, such as double walls with air space between them, flame-arresting vents, and spill-containing shelves. They shield the contents and their vapors so that they are far less likely to fuel any fire that might start in the room.

Plumbing

If you spend much time in your garage, you'll appreciate having running water and perhaps even a bathroom. The best time to install them, of course, is during the initial construction. But retrofits are possible, especially in an attached garage that either includes a laundry area or is a wall away from one.

A spacious utility sink with two faucets can help turn a garage into a potting shed or a crafts center. With two faucets, you can leave a hose hooked to one and still wash your hands under the other. Or two people can wash up at once.

Hot and cold water

Whether you're washing a car or the family dog, you can do it more easily and pleasantly with warm water. Avoid worries about whether the pipes might freeze by installing freezeless mixing valves through the connecting wall to water lines in your house. The inlet pipes on these valves slant downward toward the interior, so they drain automatically when you close the tap. The inlets are available up to 24 inches long, enough to reach well within the heated space.

Sinks

Adding a sink is more complicated because you need to tap into your house's wastewater system, not just the incoming water supply. If a soil stack (a vertical vent pipe for the wastewater system) is nearby, you may be able to connect the sink drain and vent into it. (Check your local building department and Sunset's *Complete Home Plumbing* for more information.) If this connection is not possible, adding a sink becomes much more difficult.

Utility sinks: If you do add a sink, consider a utility type rather than a kitchen outcast. Standard utility sinks *(opposite page, top)* are deeper and sometimes wider than kitchen sinks, so they're easier to use if you're filling buckets or rinsing large items. Some styles drop into a countertop, while others rest on legs or bolt to the wall. One deluxe utility sink *(opposite page, bottom)* has holes that allow you to attach two faucets, which can come in handy for special attachments, such as a bottle washer if you brew beer or a watering hose if you use your garage as a potting shed.

Mop sinks: Mop sinks, or service sinks, show up mostly in janitorial closets. A floor-mounted type can be very useful in a garage if you need a place to wash the dog or scrub lawn furniture. If you use a mop sink to fill heavy buckets, you'll need to lift them only a few inches, not feet. You may want to connect the spout to a hose or add a spray faucet.

Restaurant sinks: Restaurant-style sinks also make great garage sinks, especially if you do lots of rinsing. Most have three deep compartments to meet health department rules for food establishments. Fabric artist Carol Olsen's sink *(above)* includes a spacious, built-in drain board and a tall backsplash. Olsen went to a restaurant-supply company for the spray faucet.

Toilets

If your garage is below your house or in a separate building, you might also want to add a toilet. There's one relatively simple way to do this: get a composting toilet. Although some jurisdictions forbid them as primary plumbing fixtures in new houses, nothing keeps you from enclosing one in your garage. Buy a model with the composter below the seat. Vent it as the manufacturer recommends. With the model shown at left, that means no horizontal duct, no more than three 90-degree elbows, and a pipe that extends 2 to 3 feet above the peak of the roof.

Electricity

A bare-bones garage has an overhead light or two, an outdoor light, and at least one electrical outlet. But your garage will be safer and easier to use with a few more features.

GFCI

GFCIs

If your garage lacks ground fault circuit interrupters, make them your first upgrade. A GFCI, usually built into an outlet, monitors current flowing from the hot to the neutral wires. If there is an imbalance, which could mean electricity is flowing through a person, the unit shuts off the circuit almost instantly. Adding a GFCI to the first outlet in a circuit protects all those down the line.

More outlets

If you often use extension cords or find yourself plugging in and unplugging tools because you don't have enough slots, you probably need more outlets.

Extend an existing circuit so outlets are where you need them—at the minimum, inside and outside every door and near your workbench.

Wherever you need several tools plugged in at once, convert a standard receptacle to a double duplex, which has space for four plugs. Also consider adding a light switch above your workbench. If you adapt the idea shown at left and add pegboard where there is a box, use an extender to bring the box flush with the front of the pegboard.

More circuits

If your breakers trip or fuses blow regularly, or if you plan to add a dust collector that will run simultaneously with other power-hungry tools, you probably need an additional circuit or two. (Read the following sections to determine whether you must first add a subpanel or bring in more power.)

■ Stagger outlets so that every other one is on one circuit and alternate ones are on another. Then, when you need to use two tools at once, you can easily plug them into separate circuits. This reduces the chance that breakers will trip.

■ If your garage is drywalled, encase the new wiring in metal conduit so you don't have to snake it through the walls.

Subpanels: A subpanel *(below)* takes power from the main panel and distributes it to a group of circuits. Adding one to serve the garage solves several problems.

■ If you have a detached garage, it allows you to meet code requirements for having more than one circuit there.

■ It allows you to add circuits when your main panel is full.

■ It saves you from walking so far to reset a breaker or shut off power for tasks such as replacing a fixture.

■ If your main panel is far from your garage, a subpanel fed by a large wire will reduce the amount of power wasted on the way to the garage. Thick and thin wires may carry the same amount of current, but thick wire is more efficient because it offers less resistance. More power will wind up at the garage outlets, so tools should get the voltage they need to operate properly. This will help them run better and last longer.

■ If the subpanel has a breaker switch, you can use it to shut off all garage circuits at once.

Upgraded service: If you have an old house with outdated electrical service, you might need to bring in more power before you can upgrade the garage. An electrician can help you evaluate this. When you calculate your power needs, don't just add up the amps drawn by each piece of equipment you expect to buy. The key is how many pieces you will run at once.

Phones and security

While you're upgrading your electrical system, it's a good time to make other wiring changes as well. Possibilities include a phone line, wires for an intercom linked to the rest of the house, and a television cable. The garage shown above has a TV set on the opposite wall, but everything else is grouped in one area. Besides an intercom, light switches, and a thermostat for the in-floor radiant heat system, there are an emergency flashlight, a store of batteries, and a battery tester. (The refrigerator and freezer are elevated above any vapors that might leak from the house's gas boiler.)

Sound control

Forget egg cartons and foam mattress toppers. There are more
attractive and effective ways to control sound. Your goal may be
to spare neighbors from your tool noise or the low frequencies
of your child's bass drum. Or it may be to keep street noise out of
your office space. Either way, the same principles are involved.

How sounds transfer

When you switch on a noisy tool or turn up the music in your garage, sound waves travel out in all directions. If there are gaps around the garage door, some of the sound passes right through, into the neighborhood. Other sound waves hit interior surfaces. Single-pane windows, uninsulated garage doors, and walls that are either unfinished or covered with a single layer of drywall all begin vibrating too. The drywall makes studs vibrate, and they in turn make the exterior siding move. Soon the whole building is rocking and rolling. The motion generates sound waves that can travel well beyond your garage. Effective sound control usually involves sealing cracks and isolating interior surfaces so their vibration doesn't transfer to the exterior.

Sealing cracks

Every sound-insulation project should begin with the sealing of all air leaks, including those between sheets of drywall and around heating and plumbing holes. Some experts consider air sealing the cheapest, most effective measure you can take. Use acoustical caulk, if possible, because it contains sound absorbers and remains especially flexible, which is good for dampening sound waves. Stuff large gaps with caulk backer rod (a flexible foam rope) and then caulk over that.

Doors and windows

Sound can stream out of your garage through single-pane windows and uninsulated garage doors. If you're serious about controlling noise, replace them with double-pane windows and insulated doors, or ones made of solid wood. Doors that roll up in segments let more noise through than single panels that tilt up.

ABOVE: The owner of this garage began by replacing the garage door with a wall and double-pane windows. He filled around studs with fiberglass insulation and then nailed soundboard to the interior. (Soundboard looks like particleboard but is much fluffier.) Then he installed metal channel, which provides a ½-inch air gap. To that he attached drywall. Now, when he runs industrial-grade woodworking machines inside the garage, a person standing outside hears only what seems to be a dryer running.

OPPOSITE PAGE: There's a simple way to avoid bothering neighbors with garage sounds: confine noise to an area closest to your house. These homeowners built a wall down the middle of their two-car garage and outfitted half for their son's band.

DRYWALL

CEMENT BOARD

HOMASOTE

MASS-LOADED VINYL

More layers

Adding layers to your walls also helps deaden sound. Use different materials and thicknesses, if possible, because each combination resonates at a different frequency. Sound waves that get through one surface are more likely to be blocked by the next. For example, you might nail soundboard or Homasote, a product made from recycled newsprint, to studs and then cover that with drywall. Or install ½-inch drywall over ⅝-inch drywall. To cancel out low-frequency sounds from a bass drum, use cement board (sold as a backing for tile) for one layer. You can cut the cement board and install it between studs if your garage isn't already drywalled.

Resilient channels

To make additional layers even more effective, first install an intermediate layer of resilient channel—a metal strip that acts as a shock absorber to deaden sound. Screw channels horizontally to

studs and then screw drywall to the metal. The flexible strips allow the drywall to wiggle without transferring motion to studs. When you're done, your hand should be able to move the drywall slightly. Be careful to avoid anchoring the wall in place, even with shelf screws or brackets. If the drywall becomes fixed, it will transmit sound.

Soundproofing clips

To boost the sound-deadening effect of resilient channels and guard against accidentally locking a sound-deadening wall in place, use clips with a cushion of vinyl or other sound-absorbing material. Slide or snap hat-shaped metal channel into the clips and then screw drywall to the metal. The big issue with this system is that the clips are relatively expensive—more than $5 each—and you may need one or two for each 6 to 8 square feet of ceiling and wall.

Mass-loaded vinyl

From companies that specialize in sound control, you can buy vinyl sheeting with added barium or silica. Known as mass-loaded vinyl, this material adds a lot of soundproofing even in ⅛-inch-thick sheets. You can hear muffled conversation through a standard wall of 2-by-4 studs and two layers of drywall. But if one drywall sheet has a layer of this vinyl behind it, even shouting is difficult to hear.

SOUNDPROOFING CLIP

RESILIENT
CHANNELS

Sound-deadening drywall and plywood

Instead of trying to cobble together a sound-resistant wall from various types of sheet material and metal channels, you can buy drywall or plywood manufactured with layers of sound-deadening material sandwiched inside. These products aren't cheap, but you can use and install them *(above)* just like standard drywall and plywood. You can hang shelving, hooks, and light fixtures without providing a pathway for sound waves to transfer to studs.

Personal protection

Also pay attention to how noise affects your hearing. Sounds less than 80 decibels—about what a cordless drill makes—won't hurt you. But planers, table saws, belt sanders, shop vacs, and intense music all register above 90 decibels. This can cause permanent hearing damage, especially if you are exposed to such sounds for long periods. Hearing-protection gear will help if it has an adequate noise-reduction rating, or NRR. The higher the number, the more noise a device blocks.

■ Band-style earplugs fit around your neck. Look for ones that are washable and reusable.

■ Earmuffs work well and are easy to put on. Inspect the earpieces periodically to make sure the pads are intact. Torn pads aren't comfortable, and they let in noise.

People often like to listen to recorded books and music while working in the garage, but the headphones that come with tape and CD players don't block harmful noise. For more protection, try adding standard headphones to heavy-duty hearing protectors.

Room within a room

For the ultimate in sound control, consider building a room within your garage. On the Web, music chat boards are filled with suggestions. Basically, you need walls and a ceiling that don't touch the rest of the garage. Cover one side of each of the new room's walls with $1/2$-inch drywall and the other with $5/8$-inch drywall, using resilient channel under the interior skin. Tape all joints and fill all cracks with caulk. Add a solid-core door, weather-stripped well. And don't forget a ventilating system to bring in fresh air and exhaust stale air.

Flooring

For a garage floor, standard concrete is sturdy and fairly practical. But even when you sweep or vacuum, bare concrete never gets completely clean. It's also cold, hard to stand on for long periods, and prone to staining. If these downsides bother you, there are other options.

Plastic sheets or tiles

If you park vehicles in your garage, you may want to cover the floor with heavy plastic sheeting or snap-together tiles that withstand spills of gasoline, brake fluid, and antifreeze. A surface's design affects performance. If you want to channel dripping rainwater or melting snow out of the garage, choose a ribbed design or one with a series of holes *(below)*. If you want to roll tool cases or other equipment across the floor, pick dots or another simple design that won't catch wheels.

Wood

A wooden floor helps lessen strain on your body and keeps your feet warmer, which are big issues if you use your garage as a workshop.

Subfloor panels with molded-in cleats *(opposite page, top left)* make the job easy. The cleats leave a ¼-inch air space above the concrete so that

Carpet

If you use your garage as a play space or office, carpet will make it warmer and more inviting. Indoor-outdoor carpet is one good choice. Adhere it with double-stick tape, rather than mastic, under seams so that the carpet will be easier to remove when it needs to be replaced. Another option is self-stick carpet squares recommended for garages, which you can get in two colors to create a checkerboard design. The 20-inch-square pieces shown in the picture above have adhesive dots on the back that allow repositioning. To clean up a spill, you can pull up a section and rinse it off in a sink.

you don't need a moisture barrier. The panels are strong enough to support heavy shop equipment, even a truck. And you can leave the top surface (similar to oriented-strand board) exposed or cover it with plywood. Next to the garage door, create a threshold by anchoring a beveled piece of solid wood to the concrete with masonry screws.

You can also top concrete with a wooden floor that you build from scratch. To make it removable, spread 6-mil polyethylene sheeting across the floor. Every 16 inches, set one pressure-treated 2 by 4 wide side down. Fill the gaps between them with rigid foam insulation and then screw on tongue-and-groove plywood or oriented-strand board. Leave a $1/2$-inch expansion gap at the walls. Add baseboard to cover the gap and keep the floor from lifting.

With either method, use leveling compound or shims to compensate for the slope of the garage floor.

Anti-fatigue mats: Instead of covering the whole floor with wood, you can install anti-fatigue mats where you stand most often. Furniture maker John Thoe took this approach *(above, right)* in a way that celebrates his craft. He created wooden semicircles ringed with curved molding. Thin plywood covers the tops. Underneath, wooden supports rest on thin sheets of rubber.

Concrete toppings

Thin cement-based coatings can give a new look to a garage floor that's chipped, stained, or pitted. These toppings, designed for applications as thin as $1/16$ inch, can be tinted and left smooth or they can be stamped or rolled with a wide array of textures, some of which mimic various types of stone *(below)*. Be sure you or your contractor follows the preparation steps suggested by the topping manufacturer, especially if the existing floor has oily stains or may have been sealed. Also, incorporate existing deep cracks and expansion gaps in your design, because they will inevitably appear in any coating you apply.

Floor paint

If your floor passes the tests for coatings (see box below), paint is your least expensive and quickest solution. While hot tires soften most paint and cause it to peel, garage formulas resist this tendency. Use a water-based product to reduce the chances of peeling if moisture does come in from underneath.

Acrylic epoxies

Acrylic-epoxy paint *(right)* is one step up from standard garage floor paint in everything that matters: durability, price, and complexity of application. Though it's a one-part finish, preparation for some products requires several steps. You may need a special heavy-duty cleaner, an etching product, and a power washer, plus a special

primer coat. Follow the manufacturer's instructions. This type of paint becomes slippery when wet, so add grit, also as recommended by the manufacturer.

Can I coat my existing floor?

You might be able to coat an existing concrete floor with paint or epoxy. But test the product before applying it to the whole floor so you don't wind up with a peeling mess.

Sprinkle a small area with water. If it beads up, the concrete has been sealed. A coating won't stick unless the sealer is first removed. You might be able to use a chemical stripper, but shot-blasting (a professional job) gives the best results.

Check for moisture by taping foot-square sheets of plastic to the floor. Wait 24 hours. If water collects on the back or darkens the floor underneath, moisture is in the concrete and a new coating will peel.

If the floor was previously painted, check whether the coating bonded properly. With a razor blade, cut an X in the paint. Then rub on duct tape and yank it off. If paint covers more than a quarter of the tape, be cautious. You can strip the floor and apply a new coating, but there could be an underlying problem, such as moisture. Covering the floor might be safer.

Two-part epoxy

This is the most durable—and most expensive—paint you can put on a garage floor. If it's done right, you can drive over it, change car oil, wash the dog, and do pretty much anything without worry. Do-it-yourself products usually include a cleaner, a base coat, and color chips. The chips are plastic confetti that you sprinkle onto the wet finish to create a variegated look reminiscent of granite or terrazzo. Some kits also include a clear top coat. Products made for professional application are similar. The big difference is that pros usually shot-blast the floor beforehand for a better bond.

LEFT: Homeowner Dennis Nerstad applied this two-part epoxy floor coating himself and is thrilled with the result. If snow clings to his truck, he just waits for the debris to drip off into floor drains and then hoses down the floor.

BELOW: Although you can have a single-color epoxy floor, this type of coating is usually sprinkled with color chips while the material is still damp. This creates a terrazzo look that's easier to keep looking clean. The added texture also helps keep people from slipping if the floor gets wet.

True terrazzo

Instead of mimicking the look of terrazzo by sprinkling on colored chips, you can have the real thing. Eddie Lourenco, who owns a terrazzo company, created this smooth, elegant garage floor *(right)* by covering the concrete with a ⅜-inch layer of epoxy and aggregate, which he then sanded smooth. Here he lifts a cover over a plumbing clean-out to show the floor's layers. This type of terrazzo costs about $25 a square foot, but for a third of that, you can get a similar look by hiring a terrazzo company to polish the existing slab.

Doors

The garage door may be the biggest architectural element of your house. But unless the mechanical parts malfunction, you may never think about changing it. Perhaps you should. Besides improving the appearance of your home, a new door could make your garage more pleasant to use. There are many styles, each with advantages and disadvantages.

Sectional roll-ups

Sectionals that roll up in four or more pieces are the most popular type of garage door in the United States. They're easy to open and don't require a clear space in front—an advantage if you live in snow country. However, if your garage has a low ceiling and needs a tall door to accommodate a large car, you might not be able to use this type because of the overhead clearance required. With curved track, the minimum is generally 11 inches, although low-headroom mechanisms need only 3½ inches (plus 2 inches if you add an automatic opener).

Sectional roll-ups were invented in 1921. Simple types, with panels that are either flush and unadorned or dressed up with picture-frame panels, are historically accurate for many houses built since that time. However, these simple styles may not always add much to the look of a house.

It's possible to add windows to a standard wooden roll-up door without replacing it. You can replace the top panel. Or do as woodworker David Beyl did. He simply cut openings in the panels and added glass, which is held in place with wooden molding. Underneath, he tacked up 1950s posters explaining the use of hand tools.

Carriage-house styles: You can also get sectionals made to look like carriage-house doors. Instead of swinging open on hinges as the originals did, they move up on a curved track, just as standard sectional roll-ups do. Purists note the faint lines where individual panels join. Panel dimensions may also limit proportions on the door design, though some manufacturers make the top panel deeper than the others to create a more authentic look.

Other vintage styles: You can also get roll-up doors that don't mimic all the details of carriage-house doors but still borrow architectural details from period houses. Instead of emphasizing horizontal lines, as traditional roll-ups do, the doors shown below have a more vertical look. As with all sectional roll-ups, however, lines still mark where individual horizontal panels meet.

ABOVE: When traditional roll-ups include windows, they typically fill the entire top section. To add interest, do something a little different, as architect Bernie Baker did on his garage.

Walk-through doors: If you usually just walk in and out of your garage and only occasionally need the door open, you might want a sectional roll-up equipped with a walk-through door *(above),* also known as a wicket door or a pass door.

Roller doors: For a door that requires no clear space other than a little head-room immediately behind it, consider an industrial-style roll-up. Also known as a rolling shutter or a coil door, it consists of thin slats that wind into a compact storage box mounted over the door. This type of door is often found on commercial buildings. In residential settings, it looks best with modern-style architecture. Roller doors intended for commercial use may lack some safety features of standard garage doors. Ask before you buy.

Sliding doors

Barnlike sliding doors *(right)* move on tracks mounted over the door opening. Unless the garage is wide enough so that you can slide both doors at once, you'll need to stack them on two tracks and open only one side at a time. You can't use an automatic opener with this type of door. The advantage is that the doors do not intrude on garage space.

Swing-out carriage-house doors

Authentic carriage-house doors *(below)* swing open on hinges. They work with automatic openers, so they can be just as easy to use as sectional roll-ups. Swing-out doors don't require clear space overhead or within the garage, but they do need space in front so they can open. Your driveway must be long enough for you to park a car while leaving this clearance.

ENJOYING

YOUR GARAGE

Once you've cleaned out your garage and added other necessities, you may decide to go a step further and create a comfortable space in which to pursue your interests. The possibilities are limitless. This chapter explores many options and shows how others have solved some of the same issues you may encounter. But be sure to check with your local building department before starting any major conversions, particularly if you plan to run a business or will no longer be able to park your car in the garage.

Garage showcases

Collectors long to show off what they've hunted down, which is why many garages evolve into giant display cases for fancy cars, motorcycles, model trains, and more. In some households, the entire garage can be devoted to this purpose. In others, there must still be a place for recyclables, ladders, and garden supplies.

Motorcycle hangout

This garage was transformed into a place where riding buddies can work on motorcycles and just hang out, but it still needs to house things that are typically found in a garage. Paneling with a brick design covers an enclosure that screens the water heater and dresses up the back wall. New white storage cabinets hold other gear.

Color theme

The garage has a red and silver theme to match owner Jim McCauley's bike. He already owned red toolboxes, and he painted his new workbench to match. A red trash container and interlocking floor tiles in a red and silver checkerboard complete the theme.

Finishing touches

Harley decorations came from McCauley's rooting around in antique shops and old garages, shopping on the Internet, and networking with his Harley buddies. Finds include vintage signs, neon clocks, metal street signs, and Harley flags and posters, many of which celebrate the brand's 100th anniversary. But the centerpiece of the decor remains the item that started it all: a heavily chromed Harley Heritage Softail.

BELOW: Corrugated metal roofing covers one wall, giving it what McCauley considers "that Quonset hut, old-garage look."

Some garages must serve multiple purposes, but this garage has just one: It's a showcase for Ford muscle cars from the 1960s and related memorabilia.

Collecting cars

The owner, Wayne Haight, used to rent space in other people's garages to house all his cars. But when he moved to horse country, he built a big garage where the barn used to be so he could have his entire collection in one place. The high roof peak, hay lift, and top window give the garage a barn look.

ABOVE: The bright, clean interior creates an ambiance akin to that of an art gallery. But here, the objects on display include a vintage gasoline pump and posters and decals from gas stations of the past.

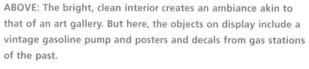

Displaying collectibles

If decor is central to the way you use your garage, you may want to adopt a trick that interior decorators use for collectibles: Group like items so you and your visitors can pick out nuances that make each piece unique. In this garage, glass shelves show off an extensive collection of model vehicles.

When you're setting up a garage as a model-railroading venue, decor isn't just a final flourish; it's the main event. David Biondi wanted his hobby to serve as a springboard to adventures he might otherwise never have. And that's just how it's turning out.

True to life

Railroad buffs like Biondi visit actual routes to measure trestles, station houses, and other details, then return to the garage to build tiny replicas—three-dimensional postcards of places they've been. Backdrop scenery, which Biondi also makes himself, is so detailed you can almost see the pine needles.

The train setup includes five tracks that snake along the walls of the garage and around a platform that rolls out into the middle of the room.

Crew jobs

Running the trains is usually a four- or five-hour event for a crew of eight, including a dispatcher who sits in the kitchen and communicates with a yardmaster via two-way radio, just as they would on a big train. Also true to form, the crew uses waybills (on clipboards below the tracks) to communicate instructions, such as to add cars to a train or to pick up a load of lumber at one stop and drop it off at another.

All aboard

Garages don't always seem the ideal place for a model railroad. When Joe Driscoll decided to build the layout in his garage, he feared moisture and dust might ruin his hard work. But he discovered a major benefit of using a garage for a hobby like this: With that big door open, the space quickly becomes a neighborhood gathering place. "Almost nightly," he says, "people walking by—some we knew, others we never met before—would stop and check on the progress of the layout. Mothers would laughingly tell my wife and me how their young boys would run a block just to see if our garage door was open. If it was, they knew I would be working on the layout and they had a good chance of watching and driving the trains."

Storage
Garages make good workout rooms in part because they're so spacious. But if yours is full, you may need to reorganize first. To prepare this garage for a home gym, the owner lined one wall with floor-to-ceiling cabinets, which he purchased through the kitchen department at a home center.

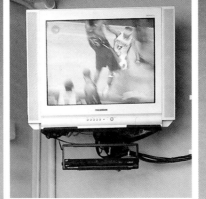

Hospitality
If you want friends to join in your workouts or simply stop by to chat, add some creature comforts, such as a soft chair.

Entertainment
A television set installed on a shelf that swivels and a sound system make workouts more pleasant.

Work area
Kitchen-style cabinets and wall hooks above a workbench corral all the tools and hardware needed for household repairs.

Exercise studios

Turning your garage into a home gym, even a simple one, may produce better results than when you have to leave home to work out. When you exercise in your garage, your schedule doesn't have to match the hours of the local gym. You waste no time in commuting. You don't need a babysitter. And you can dress as you wish and listen to whatever music you want.

Whatever your budget, it's possible to create an exercise studio in a garage. The setup here shows what you can accomplish by doing the work yourself and buying only components such as storage units. Owners Steve and Karol Schrepferman borrowed most of the exercise equipment from friends—a possibility worth investigating since people often buy gym equipment that they wind up not using or not having space for.

Bright walls and a clean floor
Steve Schrepferman began converting this garage into an exercise studio by giving the walls and floor a more finished look. He insulated the walls, then installed drywall. Taping and sanding the drywall took longer than he expected. Next time, he'll hire a pro for those steps. Painting the walls, however, was fun and easy. Coating the floor with acrylic-epoxy paint also went smoothly and resulted in a surface that doesn't chalk and wipes clean easily.

This garage shows what you can do when you set out to create the gym of your dreams. The owner, Sean Blackmore, had pieced together an earlier gym from lower-quality equipment but learned that gear aimed at the mass market isn't always best from a biomechanical standpoint. So when he set out to transform this garage, he specified professional-quality gear and set up the space so that he'd want to spend time working out.

Mirror

An enormous mirror allows Blackmore to inspect and correct his technique. The mirror also adds to the gym's spacious look, especially when the door is open. Then the mirror becomes like a giant painting, reflecting a view of the hillside across the street.

Weight training

The weight-training machine features rotating pulleys that allow Blackmore to determine his own path of motion, a key to preventing injury.

Lots of light

Halogen lights, white walls, and an epoxy-coated floor keep the gym flooded with light. A floor-coating company sprinkled flecks of color into the coating before it dried, giving the floor somewhat of a terrazzo look.

Leg exercising

To add equipment for certain muscle groups, you can invest in a multi-station gym or buy separate pieces. Taking the latter approach, Blackmore bought two leg-exercising machines: a leg press, which he uses *(below)* to build strength, and a leg-extension curl machine (shown in the foreground), to shape muscles. A multi-station would offer more options, but separate pieces are more compact and are easier to use.

Selecting exercise equipment

Before you buy anything, consider how much space the equipment needs. If your garage has a low ceiling, factor in the height you'll need for step-up equipment. You may also want to investigate what's available in used equipment. Check classified advertising in newspapers, "exercise equipment" in the phone book, and listings on the Web.

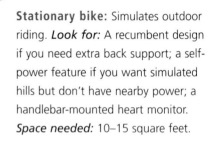

STATIONARY BIKE

Where to begin

Start by evaluating your goals. For the greatest health benefit, focus first on providing cardiovascular exercise, if you don't get it another way. Then consider weight-lifting equipment, which helps develop strength, increases bone density, and allows you to fine-tune the look of your body. If you get bored easily, factor in whether the equipment allows a range of exercises. Equipment dealers can tell you which muscles get a workout on various types of gear, but only you can judge which equipment you'll use. If you enjoy walking, you're most likely to use a treadmill. If you like skiing, an elliptical trainer or a ski machine may be better.

Ventilation

Many garages don't have windows. If the only way to provide ventilation is to open the big garage door, consider installing an operable window or two (one on each sidewall for cross-ventilation, if possible). Or add an intake fan on one side and an exhaust fan on the other.

Cardio equipment

Treadmill: Mimics walking, jogging, and running. *Look for:* A heart-rate monitor that adjusts speed and incline; a flexible deck long enough for you to stride normally; handrails; controls that simulate different experiences. *Space needed:* 30–35 square feet.

Stationary bike: Simulates outdoor riding. *Look for:* A recumbent design if you need extra back support; a self-power feature if you want simulated hills but don't have nearby power; a handlebar-mounted heart monitor. *Space needed:* 10–15 square feet.

Stair-stepper: Similar to climbing stairs. *Look for:* Your choice of independent stepping (both pedals sink when you step on them) or dependent stepping (one pedal rises when you step on the other); suitable dimensions. *Space needed:* 10–20 square feet.

TREADMILL

STAIR-STEPPER

ELLIPTICAL CROSS-TRAINER

Elliptical cross-trainer: A combination treadmill, stair-stepper, and ski machine, but impact free. *Look for:* Smooth, elliptical motion; a stride length suited to your body; handles that provide upper-body exercise or a ramp that adjusts to different inclines; programmed courses. *Space needed:* 20 square feet.

Basic home gym: Single-user gear with resistance you can set by moving a lever. *Look for:* Exercises targeted at all your muscles; a natural resistance feeling on all settings; smooth action; easy adjustability; an actual weight stack, not bands or bows. *Space needed:* 35–40 square feet.

Strength equipment

Free-weight system: Basic weight lifting. *Look for:* A solid, adjustable bench with good padding; a power cage capable of supporting the weights you intend to lift; metal or rubber-padded weights (not plastic-coated concrete). *Space needed:* 20–50 square feet.

Multistation gym: Equipment where more than one person can work out at once. *Look for:* The same features as with a basic home gym, plus easy adjustments; ergonomic features suited to your height. *Space needed:* 50–200 square feet.

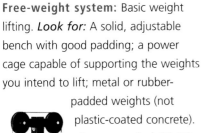

BASIC HOME GYM

FREE-WEIGHT SYSTEM

MULTISTATION GYM

Other fun and games

Besides converting all or part of your garage into a gym, there are numerous other ways to introduce exercise and fun into the space.

Climbing wall and darts

You can use a wall of your garage or even swing-out garage doors as recreational space. One advantage is that it leaves space for other activities.

You can easily build a climbing wall from ¾-inch plywood, ⅜-inch T nuts, and climbing holds, which come with bolts that fit threads on the T nuts. Or you can make your own holds from hardwood, as furniture maker John Thoe did on his garage doors *(right)*.

A dartboard on a wall or door invites a few minutes of fun between chores. Like a climbing wall, a dartboard requires little space.

Lap pool

If you love to swim, you can adapt your garage to hold a lap pool, which produces a current that keeps you swimming in place. Because of the humidity and moisture, however, some preparation is involved. For the garage shown here, the work included:

■ Sectioning off a 12-by-18-foot area to create space for a pool 9 feet wide and 15 feet long, plus a walkway around two edges. This left room for cars and storage at the other end of the 32-foot-long garage.

■ Covering the walls with greenboard, a moisture-resistant type of drywall, and painting it.

■ Adding two skylights, which open to release excess humidity and heat. A window in one wall also provides ventilation.

■ Omitting a ceiling, allowing more air circulation. This also created storage space within the trusses for a collection of vintage surfboards.

■ Providing a chlorine-free disinfection system. Besides making swimming more pleasant, it allows the pool to be siphoned out to irrigate landscaping when the water needs to be replaced every six months.

■ Adding a 220-volt circuit for the motor that makes the current, a 110-volt circuit for the water-treatment system, and a gas line for a heater.

Sauna

A sauna takes much less space than a lap pool. You'll need few, if any, alterations to your garage. No plumbing is needed; just fill a bucket so you can splash water on hot rocks to create steam. But you will need a gas line or a 220-volt circuit for the heater. Companies sell saunas as small as 3 by 4 feet, but units that size seem like closets and can feel claustrophobic. Better options, suitable for up to six people, are 5 or 6 feet wide and 7 feet long.

Besides building from scratch, you have several choices:

■ Small modulars, suitable for one or two people, arrive at your garage in halves that you can clip together in minutes.

■ Preassembled saunas come with the walls, ceiling, benches, and other parts already built. Fastening them together may take several hours.

■ Kit saunas consist of precut but not preassembled parts for finishing the interior: wood paneling, benches, a door, flooring, and perhaps a heater and accessories. You or a contractor can build the basic frame from 2 by 4s, insulation, and other materials that you buy separately.

Pingpong

If you have teenagers, adding a ping-pong table can help turn your garage into a place where they and their friends want to hang out. The table measures about 5 feet by 9 feet, and you'll need clear space all around. The International Table Tennis Federation rules specify an area 46 feet long and 7 feet wide, but kids are happy with a lot less. Tables that fold up and roll on wheels are easiest to store flat against a wall.

Garage bands

If you've ever thought about forming a band, chances are you've also considered practicing in your garage. But converting a garage to a practice space is more complicated than some of the other transformations explored in this chapter. Sound control is paramount for both you and your neighbors.

Layers of glass and air

Windows in the garage stop more sound than regular double-pane units because they consist of one layer of standard glass and one of laminated glass, separated by a space filled with argon gas and rubber edging. In this window, which backs up to a storage lean-to, the interior pane tilts slightly downward, which helps reflect sound waves back into the room and toward the floor.

Isolated walls and floor

To keep low bass notes from spreading out into the neighborhood, the interior floor and wall surfaces in this garage don't touch each other or any exterior surfaces. Hard rubber pads separate the old concrete floor from the new flooring, most of which is covered with carpet. Two layers of drywall separated by metal channels cover the ceiling and walls. One layer is ½ inch thick and the other ⅝ inch thick, so they muffle different wavelengths.

Music history

Fun touches abound in this garage, owned by Dick Weyand. Many of the instruments are vintage models, such as this red Mosrite guitar, one of about 50,000 made in the 1950s and '60s by a Bakersfield, California, company that began in a garage. The window next to the storage shed frames the headquarters sign from San Francisco's famed Winterland Arena. Weyand got the sign from a friend when the concert hall closed in 1978. The ridge beam was salvaged from the old Carquinez Bridge, the link between the eastern side of San Francisco Bay and inland California.

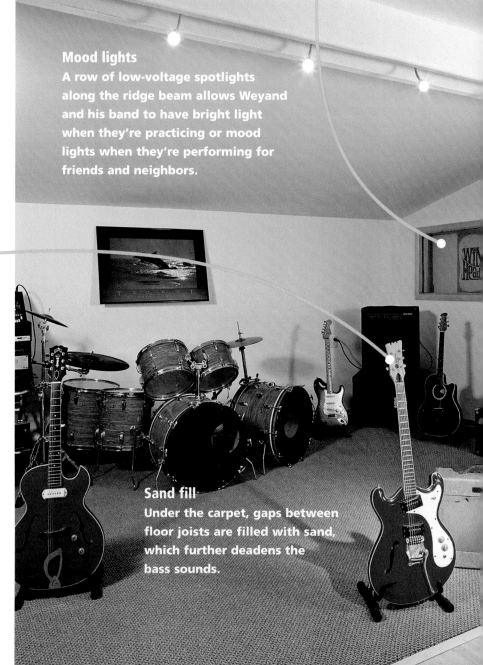

Mood lights
A row of low-voltage spotlights along the ridge beam allows Weyand and his band to have bright light when they're practicing or mood lights when they're performing for friends and neighbors.

Sand fill
Under the carpet, gaps between floor joists are filled with sand, which further deadens the bass sounds.

Dick Weyand, right, sings while playing his Mosrite guitar, backed up by his friend Dan Benson, left, an electrician who installed the low-voltage lights overhead. Weyand's brother John mans the drums.

Double doors

The garage interior is bright and newly remodeled, but on the outside, the structure looks almost as it did when Weyand bought his property in 1972. When he remodeled recently, he kept the old sliding garage door, which adds security and preserves the look of the funky old garage. But underneath, new French doors provide both natural light and sound insulation, thanks to the double-pane glass. The lean-to on the right is a storage shed. The loudspeaker on the roof is an antique Jensen, which Weyand found in an attic. When neighbors gather for parties, he hooks it up so music spreads into the yard.

Bamboo floor

A small pad of bamboo flooring serves several purposes. The band often sets up drums there because the flooring helps create a live, reflective sound. But when an audience is present, the floor often becomes a place to dance.

Dealing with neighbors

Some garage bands war with their neighbors. Not Weyand and his buddies. Their relationship is so good that when a flash flood inundated the garage a couple of years ago, forcing Weyand into extensive remodeling, neighbors and a local Boy Scout troop came out to help.

What's the secret to having good neighbors? Weyand believes it's being one yourself.

For years, his band has staged Friday night parties for the neighborhood, featuring rock 'n' roll and a fire pit where everyone roasts hot dogs. The parties often draw 50 to 100 people, including students from the nearby public elementary school, where Weyand works as head custodian and his wife, Renee, teaches first grade.

Weyand also has an open-door policy for local kids who want to make music. He invites them to record in his garage and even allows them to play his instruments, which include vintage guitars.

Home offices and studios

Whether you need a place to work uninterrupted or space for kids to do homework, your garage may make a good office or studio. But you'll probably need to insulate and add heating or air conditioning, and if your office serves a commercial purpose, you may encounter local rules that bar or limit what you want to do.

Computer setup

The owner, Leslie Krongold, edits digital videos, so she needs sophisticated computer equipment, including several monitors. She placed the computer screens on a worktable against the back wall, where she doesn't have to worry about glare.

Worktable

A second worktable faces the big garage door. Such parallel work surfaces are more efficient than one long area. Instead of straining to reach something or having to walk over and grab it, Krongold can simply swivel the chair around.

Storage options

Numerous shelving units store art supplies and reference materials. Several rolling carts are also stocked with art materials. Because the drawers are transparent, it's easy to see what's in them.

Bright walls

This office conversion began with a general face-lift. The two-car garage was extremely dark, with just a single layer of boards serving as the interior and exterior walls. But insulation, drywall, white paint, and a skylight transformed the space into an inviting base for the owner's home office and art studio.

Patio entry

Krongold's standard commute to work is through a pair of French doors built into one sidewall in the garage *(right)*. Brick paving fills in around the original flagstone pad next to the doors so she doesn't track in mud as she goes from house to work. When she participates in local open-studio days, she opens her big garage door.

Workshop area

One side of the garage still functions as a workshop for household repairs. The workbench area, near the front, includes a pegboard to keep key tools handy. Near the back of the garage, shelving units made of angle iron and particleboard store heavy equipment. Garden tools hang nearby on a rack.

Converting a garage into an office doesn't necessarily need to cost a lot or involve major structural changes. Relatively simple steps transformed this garage into a satellite office for landscape designer Marcia Bloom.

Storage and exercise

Before this garage became an office, it was a family storage area and exercise studio. The cabinets still store family items such as bulk food and extra lightbulbs. An elliptical trainer and a stationary bike remain in use.

Overhead storage

So that the garage could still hold all their general household items, Bloom and her husband added a loft that spans most of the garage, except near the ends, where the hip roof leaves little head room. A fold-down attic ladder provides easy access. Bloom hangs baskets and landscaping supplies from the beams that support the loft.

Organizer wall

Bloom wanted to look up from her desk and see something other than the inside of a garage door, so she bought room dividers at an office-supply store. On them, she mounted a lightweight shelf and a board where she keeps track of her projects.

Creative zone

Most of Bloom's computer work is done in her home office. She uses the garage space more as a creative zone to work out landscaping plans and confer with clients. She decided not to install a phone line in the garage to minimize distractions while working.

Good light

To bring natural light into the garage even when the door is down, Bloom replaced the top panel with glass panes *(opposite page)*. She paid extra for true divided lites, which have strips of wood framing individual panes rather than a grid pressed onto a large pane. Bloom also installed track lighting with halogen bulbs to give the space the feeling of an architect's or designer's office. She added task lights at the two drafting tables.

Welcoming entry

Clients often gather in the garage office, not the one inside the home. Two topiary trees, a pair of rabbit sculptures, and a mat placed in the space directly behind the big garage door create a welcoming entry for visitors when the door is open.

By rebuilding an old two-car detached garage and raising the roof slightly, owners of this property wound up with a home office and studio for their architecture and land-scape design business as well as a guest room. The new structure also helps block the view of a neigh-boring building, adding privacy to the backyard.

Open framing

To make frugal use of wood, owners John Jennings and Sasha Tarnopolsky of Dry Design used 2-by-3 studs on 24-inch centers rather than the stan-dard 2 by 4s on 16-inch centers. Plywood sheathing on the exterior adds enough strength and stiffness to compensate for the lean framing. Jennings and Tarnopolsky left the framing exposed to create the feel of a timber-frame structure. They filled in between the wood with Homasote, which is made of recycled newsprint, paraffin, and borate, a mineral that works as a fire retardant. They left a small gap behind the Homasote, which adds to its insulating value. To slightly darken its natural gray color, they coated it with a sealer that consists of linseed oil and beeswax.

Dutch doors

Custom-made Dutch doors, each 4 feet wide and 10 feet tall, let in lots of natural light, whether they're open or closed or half and half. They're wide enough so future owners could easily restore the garage as a place to park cars. Moving the worktable would open up the left stall, and scooting out a bookcase would free up the right one.

Guest quarters

A loft above the rafters has enough room for a queen-size mattress and bookcases on either side. When the space is not housing guests, it makes a great storage area.

Recycled wood

When Jennings and Tarnopolsky tore down the old structure to replace it, they salvaged as much wood as they could and used it for columns and furniture in the new space. The prize was the old ridge beam. Once they scrubbed away the grime, they saw that it was clear vertical-grain Douglas fir.

Spare and contemporary

The concrete floor, plywood paneling, and exposed wood framing give the office and studio a spare, contemporary look.

Craft artist Sandy Hogan gained the studio she'd dreamed of by converting one of her garage's three stalls.

Abundant storage space

Anyone involved in crafts knows how quickly supplies add up. This garage is ready for the load: Cabinets with shelves overhead and drawers below line both sidewalls.

Sit or stand

Countertops are set at two heights: one comfortable for sitting, the other more suitable for standing.

New windows

Hogan replaced the garage door with a framed wall that has two large windows to bring in natural light. The new windows look similar to ones upstairs, which helps the converted space blend in with the rest of the house.

Finishing touches
Bright task lighting and a built-in ironing board help distinguish this as a crafts studio, not an ordinary office. The ceiling fan keeps the space comfortable.

Dressed-up floor
A mottled green finish enhances the concrete floor.

Converting a garage to an office or studio

Here's a checklist of things to consider as you plan your office or studio. The details, of course, will vary to suit your needs.

Replacement storage: Even if your garage seems like wasted space now, chances are it still serves some useful purposes, even if it's only providing a place to park the lawn mower, stash the recycling, or hang up shovels and rakes. As you map out your office or studio, be sure to figure out new locations for those items.

Heating, air conditioning, and ventilation: Because office or studio work often involves sitting for long stretches, you'll need to provide better heating than you would for many other garage activities. To keep from wasting energy, be sure to insulate the walls and ceiling. In winter, install some type of flooring, even an area rug with a thick pad, to keep the concrete from chilling your feet and legs.

Electricity, phones, and cable lines: Try to plan for all the wiring you think you'll eventually need. It's much easier to install before you add insulation and drywall.

Work surfaces: Although horizontal surfaces in most garages tend to collect clutter, generously sized work tables or counters are an asset in a garage used as an office or studio. Adopt a policy of straightening up at the end of the day, with a bigger cleanup at the end of the week, so that you can approach each new workday with a clean slate.

Home businesses

If you dream of launching a business from your garage, you're in good company. Cartoonist Walt Disney, electronics gurus Bill Hewlett and David Packard, computer wizards Steve Jobs and Steve Wozniak, and toy pioneers Elliott and Ruth Handler of Mattel did so too. One advantage of operating a business in your garage rather than in a spare room: If customers call, they have a direct entry. They don't need to tour your house.

Family storage
If you still need to store bicycles, ladders, and garden tools in your garage, you may want to keep them close to the door. That way, you can take them in and out without disturbing your work space. This garage is a tandem double, which means it's one car wide but two cars deep. There's plenty of room behind the family storage area for Keith Bowen to run his bassoon-repair business.

Mobile cart
Secured against tipping, newly restored bassoons sit on a wheeled stand so Bowen can move them to different work areas.

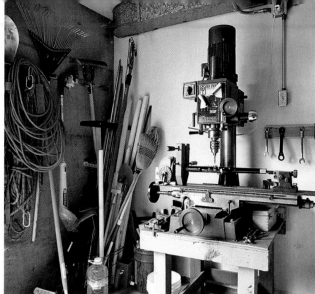

Organizing principles

The garage is organized for efficiency, which allows Bowen to work on about 500 bassoons a year. He machines replacement parts with tools set up along the right wall and mends broken metal pieces at a workbench on the left wall, where his torch is set up. At the back of his shop, next to a window that opens into the back of the property, is his finishing booth.

Mail center

If your business depends on a shipping service, an efficient mail center is crucial. Bowen, one of only a handful of full-time bassoon-repair experts in the country, keeps an old kitchen island stocked with labels, markers, and tape. On top of the stand is a stack of flattened boxes, which he ordered in a custom size that works perfectly for bassoons.

This garage houses both a wood-turning business and a school for novice wood turners. Owners Jerry and Deborah Kermode drew from their experiences in other workshops when they set up this one for maximum efficiency.

Room for everything

Two cars deep and two cars wide, the garage has enough room for four or five students to work at once. The table saw is parked near the entrance, but most other tools can be pushed against the walls or moved out as needed. To give the garage a bright, fresh look, the Kermodes added the windows and trimmed them with pine. They also installed new drywall and painted it. They salvaged the numerous fluorescent fixtures from a school remodeling project.

Tool table

With a variety of lathes, including four small ones used by students, Jerry Kermode didn't want to be constantly walking back and forth in search of tools. Instead, he loads up a cart and moves a whole collection of tools to wherever they are needed.

Works in progress

Working with locally harvested wood that hasn't been cured in a kiln, Jerry Kermode roughs out bowls and then sets them aside so moisture can evaporate before he does the final shaping. A stack of shelves near the garage door provides storage space for these works in progress. The display doubles as an enticement to potential customers, who can pick out shapes that particularly appeal to them.

Dealing with neighbors

Even when local zoning rules allow home-based businesses, running one that generates considerable noise, dust, traffic, and parking can be tricky. The Kermodes, who use their garage to teach woodturning classes and make pieces to sell, deal with all of these issues. Here's how:

■ **They don't overdo it.** Though Jerry Kermode works in his garage daily, he does so only during the daytime. One weekend a month, he teaches four or five students. Twice a year, customers arrive over four days as part of a regional open-studio event.

■ **They volunteer their time and equipment** to help neighbors who need a cut on a table saw or a hole drilled with the drill press. The Kermodes even share their tools with neighbors.

■ When they're about to make a run to the local dump, they ask neighbors whether they need anything dropped off. The Kermodes also offer their truck when neighbors need help moving something.

■ Because they're around during the day, when people who work away from home aren't, they offer their shop and home as a safe place for kids to spend time.

■ They offer to teach neighbors how to turn wood.

■ They alert neighbors to special events, such as the open-studio weekends, and invite them to visit beforehand during a neighbors-only preview.

A garage-based business tends to evolve either at the beginning of your working career, when you need to improvise and scrimp, or near the end, when you're likely to know what you need and have the money to get it. Phil McCurdy's garage is definitely in the latter category. After retiring from the Navy, he built his 40-by-64-foot, two-story structure specifically to run a business restoring vintage cars.

McCurdy's shop is a one-man affair specializing in Cords and Thunderbirds. This 1937 Cord *(right)* came to him in pieces, but McCurdy figured out where all the parts went. This was no easy feat, as Cords pioneered new technology in several ways. Besides being the first front-wheel-drive production cars, they shift gears with an unusual electric vacuum mechanism. The driver flips a switch and depresses the clutch, and the gears shift smoothly with no need for a stick.

Detail lights

McCurdy's shop has fluorescent fixtures spaced at regular intervals across the ceiling, and natural light streams in from the big garage doors when the weather is good. But he still needs more light for precision work at various tools. At this 100-year-old metalworking lathe, a clip-on task light fills the bill.

All the gear

McCurdy tries to use as many authentic parts as possible, which means he needs to store boxes and boxes of spares. Instead of trying to sort them as each box comes in, he dumps out the contents and types part names into a database on his computer. Then everything goes back into the box, which he numbers and puts on a shelf. When he needs a specific part, the program points him to boxes that have that part. The trick is to name parts in a way that he'll remember later. To help with that, he's adopted a system: All engine parts start with the word "engine," while all instruments begin with "instrument." That way, if he has to scan categories, at least some of the sorting has already been done.

"GOOD" "FAST" "CHEAP" PICK ANY TWO

The business motto, tacked to a support post.

Lined up outside McCurdy's garage are a 1937 supercharged Cord Westchester and two Thunderbirds. The blue one is a 1955 model. McCurdy bought the '56 coral one almost 40 years ago.

When your passion is your business, chances are your customers will find your spare parts and half-done projects just as interesting as you do. McCurdy's collection of parts, including these Cord horns, serve almost as decoration.

Spare bedrooms

With a little ingenuity, you can fit a spare bedroom—or even two—into a garage and still preserve space for other activities. As always, check local building rules before you proceed. In some communities, whether you add a closet or not makes all the difference in whether your changes are up to code.

This two-car garage, 20 feet wide and 24 feet long, has one stunning feature: The back wall looks out onto Puget Sound. In the distance, you can see the Seattle skyline, and behind that are snow-covered peaks in the Cascade mountain range. Katherine Kennedy and Al Kitching, who own the garage, wanted to take advantage of the view by enclosing a guest room and meditation retreat at the back. But they still needed to store their car and two long kayaks inside the garage.

Under and over

To fit everything in, Kennedy and Kitching separated the car space from the guest room with a wall, into which they constructed a box big enough for the nose of their car. Above this cubbyhole, they store their kayaks on a homemade rack, which they raise and lower with rope and pulleys.

Bed space

On the other side of the wall, the guest bed rests on top of the box. A wave-shaped wooden rail keeps the mattress in place. The bed is wider than the bump-out, so there was even room for a shallow storage cabinet underneath. Storage space is also built in at the foot of the bed, near a desk.

Desk

The house attached to the garage is quite small and has just two bedrooms. To create a home office, Kitching and Kennedy took advantage of extra space in the guest room.

Windows

The window on the right wall looks out past a huge pine tree to the water. The wide sill doubles as a tabletop when the owners pull up a chair and meditate. The window behind the bed has a view of the neighbors' living room and shower, so Kennedy and Kitching had the glass etched with an underwater scene to protect the privacy of both the neighbors and their guests.

Going up

By adding a second story to his long, skinny one-car garage, contractor Tom Spivey gained a guest room that doubles as an office. A staircase winds up the right side, using as little yard space as possible, and ends at a small front porch for the guest room. This is a neighborhood of beach cottages, so Spivey's goal was to maintain the small-scale look of the garage while still gaining more usable space from the 300 square feet it occupies.

Using the back

At the back of the narrow garage, Spivey carved out a second guest room, 12 feet by 10 feet. It has a wonderful cottage feel, thanks to pine paneling, a built-in platform bed with storage underneath, and two windows, including a generously sized window seat with a view to the back of the property.

Front view

Instead of tucking a guest bed into the back of a garage or overhead, you can place it front and center. Carolyn Brown runs an upholstery business out of her garage, so bolts of fabric, bales of stuffing, and tables for cutting and sewing take up much of the interior. But she still squeezes in a spare bed behind a door she rarely opens. The bed is elevated so she can store fabric underneath. A curtain shields the bed from the studio.

Resource guide

pg. 10, *Professional organizer:*
Eliminate Chaos, 425-670-2551
www.eliminatechaos.com

pgs. 16–19, *Garage storage system:*
Gladiator Garage Works by Whirlpool,
866-342-4089
www.GladiatorGarageWorks.com

pg. 22, *Sliding garage doors:*
Artistic Garage Doors, 650-594-1183
onsmartpages.com/artisticgaragedoor/

pgs. 28–29
Cabinet Concepts, 877-335-3664
www.customgaragecreators.com

pgs. 34–37, *Scrapbooking supplies
and instruction:*
Suzy West, www.bayareascrappers.com

pgs. 44–45, *Custom cabinets:*
Cabinet Concepts, 877-335-3664
www.customgaragecreators.com

Slotwall system:
GarageTek, 866-664-2724
www.garagetek.com

Simple shelves:
Schulte Corporation, 800-669-3225
www.schultestorage.com

Overhead shelves:
HyLoft USA, LLC, 866-249-5638
www.hyloft.com

pgs. 46–47
Custom cabinets:
Cabinet Concepts, 877-335-3664
www.customgaragecreators.com

Tall cabinets on legs:
Windquest Companies, 800-562-4257
www.homeorg.com

Steel cabinets and pegboard:
Griot's Garage, 800-345-5789
www.griotsgarage.com

pg. 48, *Wooden brackets:*
Ikea, 800-434-4532, www.ikea.com

Steel shelving:
The Container Store, 888-266-8246
www.containerstore.com

pg. 49, *Steel shelving:*
Griot's Garage, 800-345-5789
www.griotsgarage.com

pgs. 50–51, *Cabinets and drawers:*
Cabinet Concepts, 877-335-3664
www.customgaragecreators.com

Stacking bins:
The Container Store, 888-266-8246
www.containerstore.com

pgs. 52–53, *Slotwall with hidden
fasteners:*
StoreWALL, 414-224-0878
www.storewall.com

"Bulletin board" slotwall:
Windquest Companies, 800-562-4257
www.homeorg.com

Slotwall being installed:
GarageTek, 866-664-2724
www.garagetek.com

pgs. 54–55, *Metal grid system:*
Garage Grids, 877-427-2434
www.garagegrids.com

Shelf bracket for grid system:
Schulte Corporation, 800-669-3225
www.schultestorage.com

pg. 57, *Custom cabinet with pegboard:*
Cabinet Concepts, 877-335-3664
www.customgaragecreators.com

Snap-in peg locks:
The Lehigh Group, 610-966-9702
www.lehighgroup.com

Steel pegboard:
Griot's Garage, 800-345-5789
www.griotsgarage.com

pgs. 58–59, *Rigid and swivel casters:*
Lee Valley Tools Ltd., 800-871-8158
www.leevalley.com

pg. 61, *Parking aids and bumpers:*
Auto Anything, 800-874-8888
www.autoanything.com

Car turntable:
CarTurn Inc., 888-486-7946
www.carturn.com

pg. 63, *Bicycle storage:*
Brookstone Inc., 800-846-3000
www.brookstone.com

pg. 64, *Floor stands:*
Delta Cycle Corp., 800-474-6615
www.deltacycle.com

Support posts:
SportRack, 800-561-0716
www.sportrack.com

Adjustable loft:
HyLoft USA, LLC, 866-249-5638
www.hyloft.com

pg. 65, *Overhead shelves:*
Onrax Overhead Storage, 866-637-8828
www.onrax.com

pg. 66, *Mini drawers:*
Lee Valley Tools Ltd., 800-871-8158
www.leevalley.com

Metal drawer units:
The Container Store, 888-266-8246
www.containerstore.com

pg. 67, *Wooden boxes and
drawer organizers:*
Lipper International, 800-243-3129
www.lipperinternational.com

Metal divided drawers:
Lista International Corp., 800-722-3020
www.listaintl.com

pg. 68, *Stacking trays:*
Lee Valley Tools Ltd., 800-871-8158
www.leevalley.com

pg. 69, *Portable organizers, bins,
hardware cabinets:*
The Container Store, 888-266-8246
www.containerstore.com

Akro-Mils/Myers Industries Inc.,
330-253-5592, www.akro-mils.com

pg. 70, *Cabinets with shoe shelves:*
Cabinet Concepts, 877-335-3664
www.customgaragecreators.com

pg. 71, *Mechanic's chair:*
Griot's Garage, 800-345-5789
www.griotsgarage.com

pgs. 72–73, *Accessories hangers:*
The Container Store, 888-266-8246
www.containerstore.com

Schulte Corp., 800-669-3225
www.schultestorage.com

pg. 74, *Cabinets:*
Cabinet Concepts, 877-335-3664
www.customgaragecreators.com

Rolling ladders:
Putnam Rolling Ladder Co., 212-226-5147
www.putnamrollingladder.com

Alaco Ladder Co., 888-310-7040
www.alacoladder.com

pgs. 78–79, *Portable workbench:*
Black and Decker, 800-544-6986
www.blackanddecker.com

Woodworker's bench:
Garrett Wade, 800-221-2942
www.garrettwade.com

Metal bench:
Griot's Garage, 800-345-5789
www.griotsgarage.com

Hardware for build-it-yourself bench:
Simpson Strong-Tie, 925-560-9000
www.strongtie.com

pg. 80, *Custom fabric and cushions:*
Carolyn Brown, 206-842-0203

pg. 81, *Fold out bench:*
Garrett Wade, 800-221-2942
www.garrettwade.com

Murphy bed custom bench:
Cabinet Concepts, 877-335-3664
www.customgaragecreators.com

Hardware only:
Rockler, 800-279-4441, www.rockler.com

pg. 82, *"Whale" weights:*
MacNaughton Yacht Designs,
207-853-6678
www.macnaughtongroup.com

Mats with grid lines:
Olfa North America, 800-962-6532
www.olfa.com

pg. 83, *Roller glides:*
Lee Valley Tools Ltd., 800-871-8158
www.leevalley.com

Adjustable workbench:
Noden Adjust-A-Bench, 609-882-3300

pg. 87, *Magnifier light:*
Northern Tool and Equipment, 800-221-0516
www.northerntool.com

pg. 88, *Light tube:*
Solatube, 800-966-7652
www.solatube.com

pgs. 90–91, *Gas and electric convection and radiant heaters:*
Infra-Red Products Supply Inc.,
801-571-0036
www.heatersunlimited.com
www.infraredinfo.com

Enerco, 800-251-0001
www.enerco.com

Gas radiant heaters:
Superior Radiant Products Ltd.,
800-527-4328
www.superiorradiant.com

Portable heater with remote thermostat:
The Holmes Group, 800-788-5350

pg. 92, *Car lift:*
Superior Lifts Inc., 800-218-7036
www.superlifts.com

pg. 94, *Pull-down screen:*
ScreenEx, 888-368-3967
www.screenex.com

Sliding screen:
PGT Eze-Breeze, 877-550-6006
www.pgtindustries.com

pg. 96, *Powered respirators:*
Rockler, 800-279-4441, www.rockler.com

Enviro Safety Products
800-637-6606
www.envirosafetyproducts.com

pg. 97, *Cyclone collectors, reusable vacuum filters:*
Lee Valley Tools Ltd., 800-871-8158
www.leevalley.com

pgs. 102–103, *Metal safety cabinets and cans:*
Justrite Mfg. Co., LLC, 800-798-9250
www.justritemfg.com

Heat detectors:
MasterGuard, 972-393-1700
www.masterguard.com

Carbon monoxide monitor and fan controller:
Conspec Controls Inc., 800-487-8450
www.conspec-controls.com

Lockable plastic storage units:
Rubbermaid, 888-895-2110
www.rubbermaid.com

pg. 104, *Utility and mop sinks:*
Swanstone, 800-325-7008
www.swanstone.com

Kohler Co., 800-456-4537
www.kohler.com

pg. 105, *Composting toilet:*
Sun-Mar Corp., 888-341-0782
www.sun-mar.com

pgs. 110–111, *Homasote:*
Homasote Co., 800-257-9491 Ext. 1500
www.homasote.com

Soundproofing supplies and advice:
Super Soundproofing Co., 888-942-7723
www.soundproofing.org

Auralex Acoustics, 732-597-5124
TrueSoundControl.com

Sound-deadening drywall and construction materials:
Quiet Solution, 800-797-8438
www.quietsolution.com

pg. 112, *Self-stick carpet squares:*
InterfaceFLOR, 866-281-3567
www.interfaceflor.com

Snap-together plastic tiles:
MotorMat, 800-980-4727
www.motormat.com

pg. 113, *Subfloor panels:*
DRIcore Division
Longlac Wood Industries, 866-976-6374
www.dricore.com

pgs. 114–115, *Floor paint:*
DRYLOK latex concrete floor paint,
by United Gilsonite Laboratories,
800-272-3235, www.ugl.com

Acrylic-epoxy paint:
BEHR Process Corp., 714-545-7101
www.behr.com

Two-part epoxy:
EPOXYShield Garage Floor Coating,
by Rust-Oleum, 800-323-3584
www.rustoleum.com

Terrazzo and polished concrete floors:
Associated Terrazzo Co. Inc., 415-641-1995

National Terrazzo and Mosaic Association,
800-323-9736, www.ntma.com

pgs. 116, 117 bottom right, *Decorative sectional roll-up doors:*
Clopay Corporation, 800-225-6729
www.clopaydoor.com

pg. 118, *Walk-through doors:*
Designer Doors Inc., 715-426-1100
www.designerdoors.com

Roller doors:
Metropolitan Rolling Door Co.,
410-995-6336
www.metropolitanrollingdoor.com

pg. 119, *Carriage house doors:*
Real Carriage Door Co., 253-853-3811
www.realcarriagedoors.com

pgs. 132–133
Life Fitness, 800-735-3867
www.lifefitness.com

pg. 134, *Lap pool:*
Endless Pools, 800-233-0741
www.endlesspools.com

pg. 135, *Saunas:*
Sauna Warehouse, 800-906-2242
www.saunas.com

pgs. 140–141
In Bloom Garden Design
www.inbloomgardendesign.com

pgs. 142–143
Dry Design, 323-954-9084
www.drydesign.com

pgs. 148–149
Jerry Kermode School of Woodturning,
707-824-9893
www.jerrykermode.com

pgs. 150–151
McCurdy's Restorations, 360-394-3636

Credits

Photography

Akro-Mils: 69 middle right, 69 middle left, 69 bottom; **Auralex Acoustics:** 110 bottom left; **Auto Anything:** 61 right; **Behr:** 114 top left; **Black and Decker:** 78 top; **CarTurn:** 61 bottom left; **Ken Chen:** 3 middle, 76–77; **Clopay Corporation:** 4 bottom right, 116, 117 bottom right; **The Container Store:** 48 bottom, 51 top right, 66 top right, 69 top right, 72 top, 72 left, 73 bottom left; **Carrie Dodson Davis:** 118 bottom; **Delta Cycle Corp.:** 64 top left; **Designer Doors:** 118 top; **DRIcore:** 113 top left; **Laura Dunkin-Hubby:** 121 top inset, 7 top inset, 77 top inset; **Enerco:** 90 left; **Eze-Breeze:** 94 bottom; **Frank Gaglione:** 4 bottom left, 9 right, 11 right, 55 top right, 57 bottom right, 60, 85 top right, 88 bottom, 97 bottom right, 103 top right, 111 bottom right, 114 bottom left, 115 middle right, 124–125, 127 bottom right, 130–131, 145 right, 149 right; **Garage Grids:** 54; **GarageTek:** 45 top; **Garrett Wade:** 79 middle, 81 top right, 81 middle right; **John Granen:** 3 bottom, 50, 74, 93 bottom right, 119 top, 120–121; **Griot's Garage:** 79 bottom left, 47 bottom, 49 top, 57 bottom left, 71 top left; **Alex Hayden:** 2, 4 top left, 8, 9 left, 11 left, 14 bottom, 28–33, 38–39, 44 bottom, 46, 51 top left, 51 middle left, 51 bottom right, 53 bottom, 57 top, 59 top, 59 bottom, 62 top left, 63 top, 65 bottom right, 66 bottom right, 68 top right, 70 left, 70 bottom right, 71 top right, 75 all, 78 bottom, 80 all, 81 bottom middle, 82 top, 82 bottom, 83 top, 83 middle, 85 bottom, 86 bottom, 89 all, 90 right, 92, 95 top, 95 middle, 97 bottom middle, 99–101, 105 top, 108, 109 middle, 111 top right, 113 top right, 113 bottom, 117 top left, 117 bottom left, 134 top, 134 bottom, 135 bottom, 146, 147 all, 150–154, 155; **Heaters Unlimited:** 91 top left; **Jeanne Huber:** 10; **HyLoft:** 45 bottom right, 64 bottom left; **InterfaceFLOR:** 112 left; **Justrite Manufacturing:** 102 bottom left, 102 bottom middle, 103 top left; **Chuck Kuhn:** 55 top left, 117 top right, 154 bottom; **Lee Valley Tools Ltd.:** 66 bottom left, 68 bottom, 97 top left, 97 top right; **Life Fitness:** 132–133; **The Lehigh Group:** 57 middle; **Lipper International:** 67 top, 67 bottom right; **Lista International:** 67 bottom left; **MasterGuard:** 102 top; **E. Andrew McKinney:** 84 bottom right, 85 top left; **Noden Adjust-A-Bench:** 83 bottom; **Northern Tool and Equipment:** 87 bottom left; **Onrax Overhead Storage:** 65 middle; **David Phelps:** 142–143; **Norman A. Plate:** 15; **Quiet Solution:** 111 top left; **Real Carriage Door Co.:** 119 bottom; **Rockler:** 96 top; **Rubbermaid:** 103 bottom; **Mark Rutherford:** 106 top, 109 top; **Robin Stancliff:** 144–145; **Sauna Warehouse:** 135 top; **Schulte Corp.:** 45 bottom left, 55 bottom, 72 bottom, 73 top left, 73 top right, 73 bottom right; **ScreenEx:** 94 top; **Simpson Strong-Tie:** 79 bottom right; **Solatube:** 88 top; **SportRack:** 64 top right; **StoreWALL:** 52 bottom; **Thomas J. Story:** 12–13, 63 bottom, 4 top right, 82 middle; **Sun-Mar Corp.:** 105 bottom; **Superior Radiant:** 91 bottom; **Swanstone:** 104 all; **Windquest Companies Inc.:** 1, 5 top, 47 top, 52–53, **Michael Winokur:** 3 top, 3 top middle, 5 bottom, 6–7, 7 bottom inset, 14 top, 16–27, 34–37, 40–43, 48 top, 49 bottom, 53 top, 56, 58, 61 top left, 62 top right, 62 bottom left, 65 top right, 68 top left, 70 top right, 71 bottom left, 75 bottom, 77 bottom inset, 79 top, 84 left, 86 top, 87 top, 87 bottom right, 91 middle, 93 left, 93 top right, 95 bottom, 96 bottom, 98 top, 98 bottom, 106 bottom, 107, 109 bottom, 110, 112 right, 115 top left, 115 bottom, 122, 123, 126, 127 top, 127 bottom left, 128–129, 136-141, 148, 149 top, 149 middle right, 149 bottom, 121 bottom inset

Design

Advantage Fitness Products: 130–131; **Bernie Baker, Architect:** 117 top right, bottom left; **Cabinet Concepts:** 1, 3 bottom, 28–29, 44 bottom, 46, 50, 51 top left, 51 middle left, 57 top, 70 left, 74, 81 bottom middle, 86 bottom, 93 bottom right, 100 bottom, 120–121; **Butch Cleveland:** 76–77; **Closets by Design:** 20–23; **Creative Concepts Design & Construction, Tucson, Sandy Hogan and Mark Adolph:** 144–145; **Design Studios Gordana:** 118 bottom; **Dry Design, Architects:** 142–143; **Golden Eagle Construction, Daryl Rumminger:** 20–23; **Bret Hancock, Thatcher & Thompson Architects, Santa Cruz:** 63 bottom; **Roberta Lasecke, California Closets:** 4 top right, 82 middle; **Mary Jane Rehm Color Consulting:** 117 top right; **Architect Scott Wolf, Miller/Hull Partnership:** 119 top; **Thomas Spivey, builder:** 154

Index

Air conditioning, 145
Air quality. *See* Filters, air; Respirators;
    Ventilation

Bathroom, 25, 105
Bicycles
    floor rack or stand, 19, 64
    pulley system for, 63, 75
    support post, 64
    wall hooks for, 45, 65, 73
Boats, 26, 62, 63, 152
Building materials. *See* Recycled materials;
    Storage, lumber

Cabinets
    about, 46–47
    floor-to-ceiling, 26, 74, 128
    garage vs. kitchen, 29
    height, 29, 31, 44
    lighting fixtures underneath, 29, 86
    recycled, 25
    safety, 103
    supports for, 46, 47
    a wall of, 23, 26, 128
Carbon monoxide, 90, 102
Cars
    collections, 124–125
    hoist for, 60, 92
    parking aids, 61
    restoration, 150–151
Cart, rolling, 33, 42, 138, 146, 149
Casters and rollers
    about, 58–59
    glider workbench, 83
    library ladder, 74
    mechanic's chair, 71
Chain hoist, 65
Cleanup. *See* Housekeeping strategies
Cleat system, French, 55
Closets, 28, 43, 57, 93
Collections. *See* Memorabilia and
    collectibles
Containers
    bins, 37, 51, 69
    boxes, 15, 32, 67, 68
    for little things, 66–69, 70
Crafts
    home business, 34–37
    storage, 144
    work area, 20, 23, 80, 82, 144–145
Crawl space, 25, 93
Cubbies, overhead, 21, 22

Doors
    Dutch, 142
    French, 137, 139
    interior, 43, 100
    and natural light, 22, 117, 137,
        141–142, 150
    patio entry, 139
    screen, 94
    sectional roll-up, 116–118
    sliding, 22, 119, 137
    and sound insulation, 109, 137
    swing-out carriage-house, 119
    wicket or pass, 118
Drawers
    about, 50–51
    deep, 51
    dividers inside, 67
    heavy-duty, 51
    mini, 66
    padded, 18
    on steel rollers, 47
    for tools, 18, 30, 32, 51
    trash, 50
Dust control, 90, 91, 96–97

Electricity, 106–107, 145
Exercise equipment, 130, 131,
    132–133, 140
Exercise studio, 128–131

Fans
    ceiling, 145
    exhaust, 41, 95, 96, 102, 132
Filters, air, 97
Fire safety, 100–102, 142
Floor
    easy cleanup ideas, 98, 112
    in-floor radiant heat, 92, 107
    sound insulation in, 136
    water drainage, 42, 46, 115
Flooring, 112–115, 130, 136, 137, 145
Furnace, 93

Garage bands, 136–137
Garage construction, 142–143, 154
Garage showcases, 122–127
Greenhouse bump-out, 89
Grid systems, metal, 54–55
Guest rooms, 142, 152–155
Gym. *See* Exercise equipment; Exercise
    studio

Hangers, specialty, 72–73
Hazardous materials, 11, 12, 100, 102–103
Heating, 90–93, 145
Home business
    bar codes for inventory control, 36

client access, 141, 145
    display areas, 34, 36, 37
    and family storage, 35, 146
    mail center, 147
    organization, 147
Home office and studio, 138–145
Hoods, fresh-air, 96
Hooks, 55, 57, 65, 72
Housekeeping strategies, 98–99, 105, 145

Insulation, sound, 31, 109–111, 136
Inventory control, 36, 75, 150

Kitchen, mini, 82

Ladders, 45, 72, 74
Laundry area, 23, 35
Light bulbs, 84–85, 86
Lighting
    for displays, 87
    for exercise studio, 130
    magnifier lights, 87
    seeing colors accurately, 85
    skylights, 88, 135, 138
    small space planning, 89
    task or spotlights, 86, 136, 145, 150
    through door, 22, 89, 117, 137, 141,
        142, 150
    through windows, 38–39, 144, 148
    track, 87, 141
    under-cabinet, 29, 86
Lockers, 18

Memorabilia and collectibles
    display, 122–123, 125, 136, 151
    storage, 15
    weeding, 9
Metal grid systems, 54–55
Moisture in the garage, 15, 90, 134,
    135. *See also* Water drainage
Mud control, 20, 139

Neighbors
    noise issues, 109, 137
    privacy issues, 142, 153
    sharing with, 127, 137, 149
    traffic issues, 149
Noise. *See* Sound control

Office. *See* Home office and studio
Overhead storage
    between beams or joists, 31, 35, 140
    chain hoist for, 65
    cubby, 21, 22
    loft, 75, 140
    pulley system for, 63, 75, 152
    shelves, 45, 65